Janna Hellenbeck

How To Educate Your Puppy Including Training Schedule

1st edition

Table of Contents

Preface

No dog is like the other – a fact you should be aware of before you buy a dog. But even if you buy your second pet, you'll find that your dog has his own personality. That means he learns in a different way. Your second dog might be much more teachable or might even need more time to be educated.

Owning a dog means you have to be responsive to your pet. Don't try to educate your dog violently or put him under pressure, which might cause the opposite effects and your dog might suddenly develop bad habits.

Actually, there is a great deal of work ahead of you and your puppy – you'll be having a lot of fun together and will also be coming closer to each other. But always bear in mind that the mistakes you make now can cause your dog to become afraid of you in time to come.

No beginning is easy and at the very start the little one will surely miss his own dog family. That's why you need to allow for a period of necessary adjustment.

I will guide you through the subject of dog education in this book and provide you with many helpful tips. Apart from that you'll be given a "Training Schedule" consisting of 10 steps which enables you to focus on training your dog. I'm writing this book from my own experience – I was lucky enough to educate two dogs myself. Dogs are different and, such as humans. have different characters, too.

But now enjoy reading this book!

Puppy Education
– What to Expect in this Book!

If you educate your dog properly, you create the basis for having an obedient pet. I know exactly what I'm talking about. If you are in control of your dog, you might manage to avoid unpleasant and bad situations. More and more frequently there are reports to be read in the news about dogs that attacked kids, and you can't help wondering what had gone wrong. Needless to say, the reported incidents would be blamed on the poor animal. The dog would be vicious – and fairly often the pets would even have to be euthanized. But it's a fact that a dog can't always be blamed for his bad habits. Often the dog owner himself bears the very blame since he didn't educate the dog properly or the dog behaves aggressively towards him.

For these reasons, it's my advice to you to choose the right puppy education from the very beginning and start off with the basics as soon as the dog moves into your home. Every dog mom would put her puppies in their place. If they get too wild, or she simply wants to be left alone for a while, she would use her mouth to keep the puppies'

muzzle closed. Or she would use certain distinct noises that are clearly understood by the puppy.

So, the puppy gets his first basics of education from his own mom. But now it's your task to lift puppy education to another level, starting off with the subject of "housebreaking". This is the first educational step you have to take, unless your puppy is already housebroken. The next step is about leash training which is very important for the puppy while you can make sure all your walks will be relaxed.

Your dog knows who the pack leader is and feels safe. He knows that he can rely on you. Doesn't that sound nice to you? Having a friend who has got absolute trust in you and who goes through thick and thin with you.

To me, dogs are partners, and that's why they can have their own needs and own wishes. Have a closer look at a pack of wolves. Though there is an alpha wolf, they all would cuddle and snuggle up to each other. As you can see, authority alone does not mean that all those wolves with lower ranks would stay clear of their leader.

Do you realize what I'm driving at? Never beat your dog or be aggressive towards him. He will become afraid of you and won't trust you anymore. He will stay clear of you, and even if he comes up to you, he will always give certain appeasement signals and have the tail tucked between his legs. That's no friendship – that's tyranny towards the dog. No dog should be living a life like that.

Probably, everything sounds manageable to you so far, but nevertheless, you have to ask yourself a number of questions before you get yourself a dog:

✓ Have you got enough time to spare for a dog?

You have to take good care of your dog every day, that is 1 to 2 hours – for a period of 10 to 14 years. Dogs don't want to be on their own all day long simply because you're out for work. They can stay alone for a maximum of 6 hours, but there are, of course, also dogs who won't tolerate that amount of time.

✓ Which dog breed is suitable for you?

Are you an active person or do you rather prefer a cosy life? Do you have sufficient space for a big dog in your home?

✓ Did you think about what will happen to your dog when you're on holiday?

Can you take your dog with you because you pick destinations where dogs are welcome? Do you have the funds needed to put him in a kennel? - something which is not necessarily pleasant for him

Please bother yourself about those and other questions and just don't paint beautiful pictures of things. The needs of an old dog differ from those of a young dog. You might have to go walk with it every three hours in the night. Buying a dog means having to accept and take over a serious responsibility until your dog will one day cross that rainbow bridge. Do you really want a dog? Please think hard. It's a horrible fate for a dog to be put in an animal shelter in the end just because you're out of mood to accept your responsibility any longer.

Having said that, let's get started with the education. Your dog is willing to learn something – and I proceed from the assumption that you have considered everything very well and your dog will be having a great life in your home.

It's your Puppy's Turn to Learn how to Learn

Your dog must become an integral part of your family to make sure family life works out well for everybody. He must learn where his place in the pack is, and, above all, how the pack communicates with him. If your dog doesn't understand you, there can be no good family life together. He would start behaving strangely and doing things he might not consider bad at all. But you would. That's what you call bad habits or naughtiness.

It's you whose task it is to lead and guide the dog; it's you whom he must trust unconditionally, and it's you whom he must follow. If everything works smoothly, you'll become a great team. There are two different ways of learning to achieve that – operant conditioning and classical or respondent conditioning.

Let's have a closer look at these two because I suppose you might not be very familiar with them.

Operant Conditioning

If you put this educational method into practice, your dog will be fully focussed and attentive because he will be rewarded for his good behaviour. That's exactly what dogs enjoy and love. Praising him exuberantly with treats, tender words or loving care – that's what makes him feel just great. You will soon realize that your dog tends to learn much faster the things you reward him for.

That's exactly like when you are with kids. If you reward them with a cookie, they will see much more sense in clearing up their toys. That's how your dog is thinking, too. Some dogs will do nearly everything to get a treat from their owner.

Every command that you combine with a reward, will be repeated him with great pleasure. That's why you will be successful with this conditioning method even in rather hard cases. My dachshund, for example, has lived up to the reputation of his species being stubborn as a mule; and if he just didn't want to do something, he simply ignored it. However, if you would offer him a treat, it would be tempted very easily. But you should always be aware that this method of rewarding your dog is to be treated with some caution. Otherwise, he will get too fat. Best you reduce its daily feed ration in accordance with the amount of treats you give and try to substitute other rewards for them step by step. Of course, it's not a big deal to give him a treat every once in a while, but don't do it with every "Sit" command.

Your dog doesn't only learn through positive behaviour, but also through negative aspects of training. Should your dog be doing things which are undesired in your view, he must learn that he's not allowed to do these things. If you've got a dog who would constantly pull on your pant legs, remove him from it and say to him authoritatively: "No." He will be surprised and stop pulling on your pant legs very quickly.

Alternatively, you can ignore your dog whenever his behaviour is not desired. If he constantly jumps up on you, just move your body away from him without saying a word. He will soon realize that his behaviour avails to nothing and will stop it. Or command your dog to "Sit" and say "Fine" with an authoritative voice while looking at him.

This kind of education is very common and has worked out well with every dog. Now, I'm going to tell you something I will keep mentioning in the course of this book. It is simply too important to go unmentioned:

There are many dog owners who combine dog education with violence and aggressive behaviour. They would shout at their dog or hit him with leash, hand, or whatever. No way! Don't ever do it. Treating your dog like that, he won't build up trust in you. The only thing he will learn is that you're the very source of bad things, and he will become afraid of you. Dogs have a good ear, so there is no need to shout at them. They understand you perfectly well, if you speak with a low voice. Only the tone of your voice has to be adequate. It's ok, if you say "No" with a sharp voice and "Good Dog" more gently. But, surely, there's no need for you to make you voice heard all over the training ground. Hitting a dog – I stress again – is a no go for any dog education. Never wreak you anger on your dog!

Classical or Respondent Conditioning

This educational method is based on the scientific insights of the Russian Behavioural Scientist named Pawlow. As soon as a dog smells food, he starts to salivate. Humans experience the same when passing by a hot dog stand and getting the smell of it. If you use a treat to reward your dog and make the clicker sound at the same time, he will soon combine both. So, every clicking sound will immediately cause him to salivate.

Classical Conditioning is based on the fact that your dog usually learns on his own or by watching. An example: If your dog doesn't like to leave the house when it's raining, but watches you taking the umbrella, he knows exactly what's going to happen. He will turn around and resist getting out, since he knows it's raining outside. There are many examples like that: If you prefer to put on certain boots for walking your dog, he will become happy, since he combines your boots with getting outside; even if you want to go on a shopping tour without him.

Go and check what your dog's doing, for example, if he's lying in his basket. Sometimes you'll see him lying, just watching you.

As mentioned before, you can best put Classical Conditioning into practice, if you're about to start your dog training with a clicker. And it won't be long before you can stop using treats. The sound of the clicker, your verbal command or even a hint will be sufficient.

Well, I don't mean to say that you have to pick either of these two methods of learning. You should use both and combine them, when necessary, in order to ensure the best training results. But before you start off with it right away, get to know you dog first – just as your dog needs to get to know you.

Your dog's got his own personality, and even if you've had a dog already, you'll soon realize that no dog is like the other. If it's easy to distract him, you have to step up your training efforts, whereas very attentive dogs would need less efforts. If you have a dog that's bursting with energy, you have to ensure training in quiet surroundings. If your dog is a rather lazy type, you have to animate him to move. Very sensitive or stubborn dogs shouldn't be forgotten: A sensitive dog requires a great amount of empathy. Otherwise, you will overstrain and unsettle him. If your dog is a stubborn one, you need to be very patient, since you will have to keep repeating some training units for things to work well. But even in cases like that there will be occasions when your dog simply resists.

I had a Dachshund once and now I have a Chihuahua, both species known to have a mind of their own. Sometimes it's like talking to a brick wall, the dog just doesn't want to follow. Then it happens that my dog keeps looking at me very attentively and would do what I want. Unfortunately, that changes daily, and the more I get impatient, the more my dog just resists my commands.

That's why I advise you to watch your dog carefully and to learn to assess his moods in the right manner. So, you become specifically responsive to him without making him afraid or overstrain him. It may sound bothersome, but you have to do it this way and to make sure the two of you will be a good team for all of your dog's life.

"Praise" is another important subject to be observed when training your dog which will be dealt with presently.

Every Dog Needs Praise

Of course, it's only natural to rebuke your dog, a point to be covered later. But praise is the name of the game for becoming a perfect team. If you praise your dog, you signal him that he behaved as expected. That's the reason why verbal praise has to be convincing.

So be careful! The tone of your voice signals your dog the nature of the praise. If you say the words "Good Dog" with a bored voice, your dog won't consider it a praise. However, if your voice is exuberant enough, he will probably understand what you mean.

It's important for you to work flat out at the beginning, so your dog is convinced he has done something right. Later in your educational practice, you can start praising him with the words "Good Dog". At the beginning, however, it should always feel bombastic for him.

Again, it depends on you to know your dog. What treat does he love more than anything else in the world? You just have to know his favourite treat. Some dogs enjoy playing with balls and prefer a certain type of ball. In such a case, you can praise your dog by spontaneously starting a brief ball game with his favourite toy. But as my own experience goes, I can say that most dogs do an awful lot for getting their treat.

Now it's important for you to him the treat and say a specific word of praise like "Great" whenever he did something right. If that works out well, you can pick different rewards for different commands. So, there would be another reward for "Sit" than for "Down". But it will surely take some time before you can proceed like that. Optionally, you can use the clicker when rewarding your dog. As soon as he sits, for example, you press the clicker and reward him with a treat.

Generally speaking, verbal praise should always be given in connection with what it refers to. That means, don't let your dog wait for it; otherwise, your dog doesn't know what he's being praised for, which can make him become insecure, and consequently connect a treat with the wrong thing.

Praising your dog means considering one thing in especial or you might easily end up giving your praise for something you didn't want your dog to do in the first place. If your dog is a cat-hunter, for example, and if he does stay close to you obediently while fixing the cat with his eyes, you have to be really critical of that behaviour. If you give praise to your dog now, you signal him it's just great to fix the cat with his eyes. You're teaching him that his behaviour is correct, though originally you wanted him to ignore the cat.

By and by you should try to omit the reward when praising your dog. Well, that doesn't always work out well with a puppy, to be honest, but if your dog knows all the commands, you can start trying. Instead of giving a reward you can fondle him saying something like "Good

Dog"; don't forget to call him by its name. It's important that your dog feels addressed by you. Then, try to use your verbal praise sparingly and stop praising him for everything done right. Well, it's not a mistake to praise him for this or that several times a day, but don't overdo it for everything he does right. Your dog must learn that your commands are to be followed quite naturally and in expectation of a reward. That's the incentive for him to behave right all day because he doesn't know when a praise or a treat will be next.

If you want to get yourself dog as a family, it's imperative for you to agree on consistent educational practice for him. Unless you might use different words for certain commands and confuse him. Apart from that, it might happen that you praise your dog for a certain behaviour your partner might not like at all. It's like when you have kids – you just have to pull together.

Now, it's a great solution to have a dog training diary. Make notes on this or that kind of training, on when it was conducted and how it was completed by your dog. Also write down which command or words you use and which kind of reward you use to give to your dog. A dog training diary makes it easier for you, particularly if you and your partner don't walk him or are training with him together.

Let's now come to the question how to rebuke a dog because that's also part of every good training.

Rebuke – But do it Right

Watching your body language and hearing the sound of your voice, your dog will notice that he's done something wrong. However, he will behave like that only if he knows you more closely. At the start of your training, he won't be aware of the fact that he keeps nibbling at your shoes. Take the shoe away from him, look at him intensively and say "Fie" and his name. It's no big deal, puppies learn from their mothers' what rebukes are. If the puppy does something the mother doesn't like, she will grab his muzzle with her mouth. Doing that, she's snarling, and the puppy will know exactly that his mother doesn't like what he's doing.

Now it's up to you to show your puppy what he's allowed to do and what he's not allowed to do. If he wants to be in your bed very badly, and you don't want him to be there, you have to say "No" to your puppy with a strict voice while grabbing him in his neck fur and pulling him away. Never shake your puppy, shove him away or even throw him off the bed. Playing puppies often get fairly rude and would snatch after hands and feet. Grabbing him by the muzzle and uttering a strict "No" can be very effective in such cases. But never use force to squeeze your puppy's muzzle.

A rebuke can be considered most effective if a dog understands immediately – but he should become afraid of you. So don't shout at him and don't hit him with your hands.

Always stay consistent in what you do. Some dogs can have enormous stamina if they want something badly. You might have to repeat that bed-game several times in a row, perhaps even night after night. If you give in just once, you'll be faced with the problem that your dogs won't understand you anymore. Why is he never allowed to do it, and why right now? This kind of confusion can make your dog disobedient, and he won't accept your "No" as a "No" anymore.

The surprise effect is very effective, too. If he barks at the garden fence, throw a can filled with screws on the ground next to him. The metallic clang will scare him, and if you keep doing it, he won't be standing at the fence sooner or later. Well, he won't realize that it's just an educational measure because he won't connect the can with your person. In the very moment he barks, he wasn't focussed on you. That's why he doesn't realize that it was you who threw down the can with screws on purpose.

By the way, there are several "training tools" which can be quite helpful. There are collars with an inbuilt water reservoir. As soon as the dog starts barking, he's being splashed with water. That's fairly practical, if your dog is a real barker and if you're not at home. He will learn swiftly that he's better off not sitting in front of the door barking. However, I would recommend that tool only if there is no other alternative to make your dog learn to behave right. As long as you're in with your dog, you can always signal him with the "Leave it" command that he's to stop barking at the door. In case of doubt and if your dog won't stop, you can consult somebody at a dog school. In most cases, dogs that are left alone too quickly in life develop that kind of behaviour. That's why you should teach him to stay inside as early as possible or your neighbours might complain about his barking sooner or later.

I disapprove any training tools that make use of electric shocks. It's simply cruelty towards animals because they inflict pain on the dog. Of course, the dog won't connect the punishment with you because it's not you who is hurting him. But, anyway, those tools can make a dog aggressive in the worst case. Such tools are, for example, available for garden use. The dog wears a collar, and the sensors of the tool are stuck into the soil covering a certain area. If the dog moves too far leaving the perimeter of the sensors, he will be given an electric shock. These "things" are meant to teach the dog to stay within certain domestic boundaries even if the gates are opened wide. In my view these "things" are barbaric and not animal-friendly. Think of your kids. You would certainly prevent them from running away from your house by means of a fence and a door and wouldn't punish them with electric shocks.

Now you know that there must be praise and rebuke alike. But everything has to happen kindly and without aggression and violence.

Learn to use your Body Language

Among the members of their pack dogs don't communicate by means of sounds, but mostly by means of their body language. That's why your dog will always be watching you closely. Your body language tells him a lot. Needless to say, it's to your disadvantage, if you make improper use of it, thus telling your dog something you don't want to communicate.

Remember that by watching your body language, your dog can detect that you are insecure. That's the reason why you should always act securely and positively in his presence. If it works, he will accept you as his guide because he feels that you give him safety. However, if you are heedless or if your body language is not in keeping with what you say, your dog will be irritated. Dogs dislike insecure behaviour which only stirs them up to do what they want. He learns that you're not his guide and that he's bound to decide for himself. In extreme cases, dogs can even try to take over control. He won't accept you as the leader of the pack any longer and will try to become the boss himself.

You have to watch your body language while training your dog. If you train the "Sit" command, for example, you want your dog to remain calm, which means, however, that you have to remain calm as well. Your body language should be calm, so crouch down next to him, embrace him carefully and fondle his breast while you praise him verbally. But remember, there are dogs that don't like that.

If you want to prevent your dog from doing something, just make yourself big. Look at him with a stern face and adjust your voice. But should you want to call your dog to come up to you, and he follows your command in a slow manner, you can't obviously proceed like that. Otherwise, you would but irritate your dog and signal him rather not to come up to you. Be careful with this body language – never pose like that in front of a dog you don't know because he might possibly consider that a threat and attack.

Another example: If you train the command "Sit" with your dog, proceed as follows so he can understand you: Say this command and, at about breast level, point upwards with your finger. The dog must look up to you to follow your finger while, quite automatically, his bottom will move almost on to the ground. Now finish up your "Sit" training by first exerting some light pressure on his hindquarters. Then, you command "Sit" again and give him treat and verbal praise. If you command "Down", you make a downward movement with your open hand. You might have to train the "Down" command out of the "Sit" command at the very start of your training sessions. To be successful, you command your dog to sit first, then you softly pull his fore paws forward so he will lie down.

It's important that you remain completely calm when doing these exercises with your dog. Well, try to be as calm in all you do in your life. Should your dog notice that you're stressed and have a nervous body language, he will become stressed, too. Some dogs get nervous and don't know what to do, while others are irritated in such a manner that they withdraw fearfully into their basket not knowing what is going on.

If you have kids, your kids should learn that, too. Needless to say, they have to be old enough to understand what they're doing. Having toddlers, you better reserve a special room for your dog where he can withdraw if things get too wild. Kids can easily stir up a puppy. He gets restless and plays along, the problem being that he only enjoys it because the kids enjoy it. So, he learns that their behaviour is good, and in later years, you've got a grown-up dog at home who just behaves crazy. It can be quite bothersome, if you have Chihuahua – but imagine it's a grown-up German Shepherd that jumps and leaps all over the place. That's far from being funny! And that's why you should remove your puppy from the action every once in a while, and let him have his nap in a quiet place.

Which brings me to the next subject – your voice, being the most important tool when educating a dog.

Using your Voice Properly

Not only do dogs adjust their behaviour to the human body language, your voice is an important training tool as well, and you shouldn't underestimate it for your work. That's why I mentioned elsewhere that you should never shout at your dog. Body language and voice have to be in keeping with each other.

You just can't be open to your dog and command him to come, if you say "Come" with an authoritative voice. That doesn't fit together. The dog sees your open and inviting body language, yet hears a vocal sound that doesn't promise anything good. That makes him insecure, he doesn't know if it was really meant to command him to come or if he's about to be scolded. Even if you talk to your dog very lowly, he can find out, if it's worth for him or not, by judging your intonation and your body language. Remember that your dog's hearing is very refined and that he can hear even the lowest sounds.

Please avoid talking to your dog all the time. There are dog owners who consider their dog their spare child or a substitute for a partner. The dog is chatted up all day long, which might be quite pleasant for a human being, but your dog can't make anything out of all those words. Sooner or later, he will start ignoring the voice talking to him and won't follow it any longer. The consequences for you will be rather unpleasant, since your dog won't do what you command him to do. He simply won't react anymore, and all your educational efforts will be useless.

If you talk to your dog, always be brief and succinct. If you command him to lie down, it's sufficient to say "Down"; if you don't want him to do something, just say "No" to him with a gnarling voice. There's no need for you to talk in eloquent terms to your dog because he won't understand words other than those, he knows to be commands.

Watch the tone of your voice whenever you speak. Your dog will detect, if it's joyful and friendly or malicious and unkind. He knows well how to differentiate between a praising or a rebuking voice. Using a monotonous voice is likewise disadvantageous because you might be bored, and your dog won't be able to find out what it means. He won't react to it.

Use your voice as skilled as your body language. Your dog will love to hear and follow it. That also means a lot of training for you because it can happen that you have to change from a friendly voice to rebuking one.

One example: You command your dog with a joyful "Come" to come up to you. His reaction is swift, but while running to you he suddenly detects a hare which he wants to chase. So, it's your turn to chance from your joyful "Come" to the rebuking "No" command.

That might not be easy to do, and you should therefore rehearse it without your dog. It's a fact that your dog, if he follows you well, is able to differentiate between those commands and know right away that he's not allowed to chase the hare. It's all up to you then to change to a friendly "Come" command again. That's not that easy, if you're upset at the thought that he's chasing a hare. So, you realize that your dog can teach you a lot, too. That's why things only work out well, if the two of you cooperate and learn how to communicate with each other.

Of course, it gets more complicated, if more than one person looks after a dog. It can happen that the dog will comply with the commands of just one person while others, for example, will have to use the leash when walking him. But it also depends on the dog. If he's well educated, knows all commands and feels safe, he might overlook a flawed communication.

My Dachshund, for example, was educated by myself and we were always together in the field. When I was at school, my father looked after him. We had divergent views concerning dog education, and being with my father, the dog was allowed to do many things I didn't like at all. Unfortunately, they didn't communicate very well, and my father would be quick to shout at the disobedient dog. The dog, on the other hand, ignored it with a certain coolness - he ignored everything my father said. But, surprisingly enough, he could walk the dog without any problems and the dog would go behind him or alongside with him. And he didn't even use a leash. My Chihuahua, on the other hand, complies nearly perfectly to my intonation. If I'm stressed and use the wrong tone in my voice, he would draw in his tail and withdraw into his basket, even though it's not my intention to scold him. As you can see, I have to be careful and watch my words. Dogs react differently and my Chi is a sensitive soul.

As we are on the subject of voice and speaking, let's come to another related subject: Address. Even a dog wants to be addressed so he knows you mean him and not anybody else. Well, many mistakes can be made when addressing a dog.

To Address a Dog

Well, your dog can hear you talking, but he won't bother taking notice, since it's nothing out of the ordinary. He quickly learns to understand his name and will react when being addressed with it. But sometimes he might not feel addressed because he's simply not up for it.

Address your dog like you address a human being. Look at him, speak out his name and let your body language show him you're focussing on him. He will look at you, prick up his ears, be attentive and anticipate something nice from you. It can be a treat or your call to go out for a walk.

When talking to your dog, always make sure that he feels addressed by you. That's of foremost importance when training your dog. If your dog is absent-minded and is looking elsewhere, you can't simply expect him to execute your command straight away.

You can make young dogs look at you by holding a treat in your hand. In most cases, however, they are so distracted by their environment that it's hard enough to get their attention. But it works well, if you have a treat. Get started with your training or game only if your dog is looking at you. Then he will be all ears.

What's the Point in Educating a Dog?

Of course, you have good reason to put this question. Everything would be so easy, if you wouldn't have to work hard with your dog. Going for a walk, huddling together and perhaps playing for a short while, that sounds quite easy. Always remember that your dog is like a kid. If he doesn't know what he's allowed to do and what he's not allowed to do, he will do a lot of things you won't like.

The dog mother starts educating her puppies when at a very young age. But she does so up to a certain point. At a certain time in their lives, the puppies break loose from their mother and become an integral part of the pack. They have their appointed place in the pack, and, quite naturally, they would also be rebuked by the others, if something is wrong. But things like that happen in the pack of dogs. Of course, that kind of dog education can't be the same in a pack of humans.

You have to show your dog the right way to do things. He must learn the things he's allowed and not allowed to do in his new pack. First thing is the puppy must learn to make his business strictly outside the house and not on the carpet. A young dog can come up with really strange ideas, I can tell. They would chew at the edges of your furniture when it's time for tooth replacement, bite shoes to pieces or tear cushions apart and much more. You won't believe what strange ideas a dog can have.

My Dachshund, for example, knew how to open the shoe cabinet. Every time I was out, he would really go for the shoes and pull them out of the cabinet. But the crux of the matter was that he would bite to pieces only one shoe of a pair. So, it was not long before that I had many single shoes, but no pairs anymore. The whole story ended when the cabinet was eventually locked up. Strangely enough, he would leave undamaged all those pairs of shoes that were outside the cabinet. When my Chihuahua was still a puppy, he began cleaning the cat's tray one day. He would usually get the excrements out of the tray and put them in some corner in the house.

You see we're dealing with nasty dog habits; you certainly want to drive out very quickly. They're simply not nice. Both dogs had to learn that they must not do it. Until today, my Chi stares spellbound at the cat's tray, but he knows exactly that he's not allowed to remove things from it. Sometimes you can really see how hard it is for him to resist. I used to waylay him when he came sneaking into the bathroom. The moment he wanted to get into the cat's tray, I commanded "No" with a strict voice. After five attempts he would turn around swiftly the moment I addressed him "Felix".

Needless to say, you wish your dog to participate actively in your daily routine or your family life. But that works only, if your dog was educated properly. He must learn to deal with the stimuli of his environment, for example, with street noises, other dogs and big crowds of people. Apart from that, you have to rely on him. If your dog misses out on that, he will get stressed very quickly in certain situations and might even get aggressive.

You can train a lot of things with your dogs. But it takes time. It's absolutely ok, if you want to restrict your education to the necessary basics. It's important for both of you that he learns to obey your command to come, not to pull the leash and to sit and lie down. Also, he must learn to stay alone at home, not to jump up at people, that he's not allowed to beg for food at the table and that the right place for his business is strictly outside the house.

Applying these basics, you will be on the right track, and you will also have the chance to expand your educational measures when need be. But now there is the question when exactly your dog should know how to do certain things. Well, that depends on the species as well as the age of your dog.

As a rough guide, you can say that a puppy should know how to do the following things by the end of the fourth month. He should:

- ❖ be housebroken, night and day

- ❖ know his name and react to it

- ❖ come up to you, if you call him

- ❖ "Sit" quietly

- ❖ stay down at the command "Down" for at least a minute

- ❖ comply with "Sit" and "Down" commands without the need of a treat

- ❖ walk short distances on the leash

- ❖ turn around to you when walking him

Well, you can't generalize how fast and well a dog is able to learn to behave like that, but he should at least be trained to know the above-mentioned basics. It could well be that he won't be able to comply with all of them in the beginning.

Always bear in mind that your dog will outgrow his puppy age towards the end of the fourth month and then enter his adolescence. Now, it's starting to be wild, and you will have a teen dog in your house that's willing to try to find out who's in charge. There are dogs that start to question everybody and everything for which reason you'll be well advised to have successfully completed some parts of your dog educations by then. He will have a clue who's in charge and will have built up the necessary amount of trust in you.

Educating a dog, you have to be mindful of the special demands of the dog species. Having a Jack Russel, for example, you can't expect him to stay quiet for a long time. Being a package full of energy, it's his nature to move a lot. On the other hand, you can't expect a Carlin to fetch balls for hours and hours. His body isn't simply made for that kind of activity.

That's why I mentioned at the beginning of this book that you should inquire well which dog species would be the best for you. If you prefer short walks around the house, you will get problems having a Border Collie. If body or mind, these dogs want to be challenged. Most dogs want to go for long walks. I don't know, if it's the same with smaller species, but my Chi feels perfectly content when walking around the block in bad or cold weather. If not on a leash, he would soon turn around and run back to the door of the house on his own.

But now. let's get down to work!

How to Educate a Dog?

When it comes to dog education, it's a bad thing that some people still think of drilling a dog and using violence. But that's exactly what dog education should never be! You must never drill your dog and, above all, must never shout at him or beat him!

Educating a dog is about working together with your dog. He must learn to execute your commands, even if he's absolutely not in the mood to do so. Of course, a certain amount of force is necessary because your dog would likely prefer doing something else than training commands with you.

When educating your dog, always bear in mind that he's got his own personality. If you have a positive attitude, you can motivate your dog to join in. Unfortunately, that doesn't work out well with every dog. Sometimes you might have to bribe him with his favourite toy or an especially delicious treat. But you have to have a plan and go about systematically. Show self-assertion and stay calm whatever you do.

And if your dog decides to comply with your commands but grudgingly, stay focussed and correct him. If he doesn't want to follow your "Sit" command properly, press his bottom smoothly into the right position. If you don't react to his bad behaviour, he will keep trying again. He must know that it's you who's in charge and decide about the correctness of his behaviour to comply with your commands.

Plan your training sessions on a regular basis. It's this orderliness that makes your dog feel secure. But be always sure to have a positive attitude whenever you train him. If you're in a bad mood, refrain from educating him, since your mood is transferred onto your dog and makes him insecure.

As long as your dog is still a puppy, it's sufficient to run your training session for a few minutes or so. He won't be able to concentrate on you for a much longer time anyway. If he's grown older, it's a good idea to extend your dog's training time up to one hour a day. You don't need a special training ground. Educate your dog when and wherever you like to. At home, when walking him. Just integrate the training into your daily routine.

It's highly important for your dog to realize he's been successful, something which should best be towards the end of the training session. Thus, you leave him motivated for the next time. If you train new tasks with him, always end your training session with an exercise you know your dog knows inside out. If you notice that a certain exercise doesn't work, stop it and do something else instead you know will work well.

Don't forget to think about the reasons why a certain exercise won't just work. Do you give your dog the wrong signals? There must be a reason why your dog doesn't understand what you want him to do. Try to solve the problem. If the training exercise doesn't work, it's a frustrating business for the dog as well.

Keep your dog on the leash when you start off with your education, so you can make sure that he won't run off when not in the right mood. Use a towing rope or let loose your regular walking leash. Your dog will have to feel free and off-leash, while you can still control him if you need to.

It's you - and only you - who finishes the training exercise. Your dog must learn that it's not him who decides when to finish something, but only you. That's why the passage from one exercise to another should always be fluent. And if you see he's got enough, just signal him to "Go", so he knows he can romp about again. That's an all-important point to observe if it comes to "obedience".

Especially, if it's the first dog you own, why not try out a dog school with him. The playgroup for puppies is a gorgeous choice if you wish to teach him the necessary social behaviour. You can get great workable advice regarding "training subjects", and problems you might have can be solved easily together with a dog trainer.

Since being on the subject: To walk a dog on a leash is something that needs to be trained, too. Big dogs, for example, are very strong. Of course, you must correct your dog for which purpose you've got the chest harness. If your dog tugs on the leash, you can correct him without causing injuries.

But it's no good advice to use choke collars or collars with metal rivets. These gadgets will hurt your dog. Of course, your dog would stroll alongside obediently knowing that he will hurt himself when tugging on thc least. But if your dog is off-leash just once - you won't be able to control him anymore because he was never really taught to walk next to you.

It's a great opportunity to teach your dog the "Heel" command by way of treats that you have in your pant pocket. He will walk next to you very obediently because he wants to get the treat. However, that trick works with bigger dogs only. My Dachshund and Chi were definitely too far away from my pant pocket. Well, I could have put the treat in my shoe, but that, honestly, would have been a step to far for my taste. But always watch your dog. If he stares on your pant pocket, just keep the treat in the other pant pocket where the dog is not.

I kept mentioning that you need to be responsive to your dog while training him. But to be successful, you also have to watch his various phases of learning. If you know these phases well, your training will be much easier.

The Phases of Learning in a Dog's Life

On his way from a puppy to a fully grown dog, your new friend will have to live through different phases of development. You can compare these phases to those of a kid, that is, his development from a baby to a toddler, to a teen, and later to an adult. However, these phases are considerably shorter. Take it easy - remember, you let your puberty behind you fairly quickly, didn't you?

How quickly a dog enters his adult age depends on the species. It can take up to three years before he's outgrown his teens. During that time your dog has to learn many things, and you have to become one great team. If you miss that out, it' going to be a tough job. A grown-up dog can be taught things, of course, but it isn't that easy anymore.

Everything starts when a dog is born. The tiny puppy is born blind and deaf and needs his mom. The first three weeks of his life are termed "vegetative phase". He can't perceive his environment and, basically, is only interested in sleeping and drinking.

With the fourth week after birth, your puppy enters his socializing phase. He starts to use his eyes and is more and more agile. He also starts taking interest what's around him and is off to explore his environment. Together with his sisters and brothers, he discovers his world playfully, trying out what he's allowed to do and what he's not allowed to do. His mom is his guide and educates him. Playing with his siblings, he would test who's the stronger and more daring one. During that phase you can see from the behaviour of the puppies who's bound to become a little daredevil and who's having a rather quiet character. It's in this early phase that the dog breeder or dog owner should start to make the dog become accustomed to several things. That means the puppies should be given the chance to get in touch with strangers.

That's why I strongly advise you to ascertain how a dog breeder keeps his dogs. Are his dogs integral members of a family, do they live together with human beings, or are they kept in kennels.

Generally speaking, puppies living in a family are much more open-minded because they're always together with human beings and know, for example, other people coming for a visit. Puppies raised in kennels are not very familiar with human beings, and therefore, usually show a distinct shyness towards them.

As soon as you've got the puppy in your house, that is roughly after the 12th week, it's all up to you to give him the chance to get as many impressions of his new surroundings as possible. But allow a certain time for his adjustment before you start. What he learns now, won't be a source of fear for him any more in years to come. Show him other dogs and other people. Show him kids and walk him along a road every once in a while, so he can get to know street noises.

I recommend visiting a school for puppies. It's not about teaching him things, but he's got the chance to play around and romp about with other dogs. You certainly know by now that I'm not so fond of dog schools, but the school for puppies I went to I really liked. My Dachshund could play like crazy, and I was happy not to fear he's run over by a big and heavy dog and hurt. There were only puppies there.

When dog is about five months old, he's no longer a puppy. Now, he becomes a young dog, that is a teen. If you can make full use of his socializing phase and could train your dog well, you might see the fruits of your efforts. He enters his teen years, and, believe me, he will have may stupid ideas in his head. He's willing to test his strength which means that he will shut his ears and ignore your commands more than once. If your dog knows the basic commands now, you will have less difficulty to keep him under control. It's important for you now to further extend and intensify the obedience training with your dog.

Always be sure the tasks to accomplish make sense for him, so he won't be bored. Otherwise, you might give him the opportunity to develop bad habits, like chewing the furniture. There are dogs tend to get insecure, like in cases of rather sensitive dogs. Therefore, it's important for him to have full trust in you. But you can make him feel secure if you stay authoritatively next to him. Show him that you protect him and that he can rely on. He can make that experience, if you stick to your daily routine like going out for a long walk and play games with him or fixed daily mealtimes.

Shortly before his first birthday many dogs get sexually mature. If you have a female dog, she'll be in heat and is ready to become pregnant. If you have male dog, he starts lifting his leg and looking after female dogs. Now it's time for you to watch over your dog even when walking him. If you don't want to get puppies, you have to do something to manage to keep her away from male dogs. That means, walk your dog on the leash only. Or you can go consult a vet.

All that happens next, is about the adulthood of your dog. It's no longer so easy to manipulate him and should he have stupid ideas in his mind, it will be rather hard for you to change that.

Team Leader - It's up to you to call the Tune

Have you ever wondered how a dog picks his pack leader and, basically, what makes a good pack leader? The principle of picking the pack leader is an easy procedure for the dog. Whoever looks after him, makes sure there's food and plays with him, is top in the hierarchy of the pack. Needless to say, you have to set the rules and stay consistent. That makes your dog feel secure and safe.

If you fail to do so and, if the dog lives a life without being integrated in your family, he will start to put things in order himself. He will try to become the leader of the pack, and you might end up being hurt by painful bites. For the dog it's the only way to rebuke you. But you must prevent that from happening in any case!

Make sure you command your dog to play or go outside for a walk. Never give in to your dog's demands. Of course, hc wants to get the treat now, but it's you who decides when he gets it. If you give in to his demands too often, he's about to win and will take over command. Within a pack, a subordinate dog would never demand the alpha dog to play with him or even eat first.

Should your dog show signs of a dominant behaviour, let him know where to stop. Only the high-ranking "animals", humans in other words, are allowed to lie on the sofa. Also, it's the high-ranking animals that enter a room first and before the others. Same with food. Your dog gets his food when the high-ranking animals have finished their meal. You can forbid your dog to enter certain rooms by closing the door when you're inside. Behaving like that, you show him that you're the alpha animal, not him.

I know that's hard and not unlike me, you won't like to do it, but you have to do it. As mentioned above, you might like the sudden dominant approaches of a little Chihuahua better than those of a Great Dane with his 50 kilograms and more. In that case, the cards would be stacked against you,

It's a great exercise, if your dog has to wait for the feeding dish. You can train that day after day as follows:

1. Let your dog come to you and prepare his food.

2. Before you give him his food bowl, he has to comply to the "Sit" command and stay quiet.

3. Place the food before your dog and make sure he stays quietly in this position.

4. Wait a moment, then count to three and signal him he can eat from the food bowl.

This exercise alone will show him that it's you who are the alpha animal. You provide the food, take care of your pack, and you decide who can eat at what time. You must remain resolute and consistent in what you do. If you say it's time to stop eating, your dog has to leave the food to you. Why is it so important? Imagine your dog finds something to eat on a meadow. It could be poisoned. So, you need to have the tool to stop him from eating it up. Even if he's got it in his mouth already, he must have been taught to let go on your command. You have to train that with your dog in a very painstaking way. It can save his life one day.

The Basic Education of your Dog

So far, you've read a lot about the theory of dog education. And even those subjects could be dealt with more thoroughly. But now it's time to talk about the basic education and how you proceed properly. Why it's so important, you should know by now. Nevertheless, let me repeat it: Be resolute!

There is a proverb: "You can't teach an old dog new tricks." And there's some truth in it. I never taught my Dachshund the command "Heel!". In my opinion, it wasn't that important, and somehow, I wasn't up for it myself. But it's a fact that this small Dachshund became a grown dog with a certain weight. Bennie was always in a hurry, and so he braced himself against the least and rushed off. There were times when I had to pull forcefully on the leash in order to stop the dog. But when it crossed my mind I could teach him the command in question, it was too late. He was a good pupil and had learned a lot as a puppy and teen dog, but being two years old, he simply wouldn't learn the "Heel!" command. Well, he wouldn't pull that much after a while, but on the leash he never made it go next to me the way he should have done it.

Perhaps it was my fault. Well, I mean to say that you must definitely use the first year of his life. Be together with your dog as closely and often as possible and teach him as much as you can. But don't demand too much of him! A well-educated dog is worth a mint because you can take him everywhere you go and where your dogs are admitted.

If you like, you can buy a clicker and work with it. But also get yourself some toys your dog likes to play with. But make sure that he never gets three at a time. The more toys there are, the faster they become stale for him. If need be, just take the other toys away from him and swap them occasionally. The things you don't get too often, are much more interesting for you.

You start off with your education the moment he moves into your house. Of course, he must get a feel for the new surroundings and adjust to the new humans he's in touch with. Give him time and use the time to walk your dog and focus on him. If he could settle, you can start educating him. Place a basket for him in the room where he can sleep. There is, however, no place for him in your bed. But don't let him sleep somewhere else because he hasn't been used to sleeping alone so far.

Training a dog means you proceed step by step. Some exercises are modular, that means, for example, you can't train the "Stay!" command, if he doesn't know the "Down" or "Sit" commands. If you see that your dog has mastered one exercise, you can increase the workload and make tasks more difficult for him.

One example is the "Stay" exercise: First, your dog has to sit down quietly for a short while, later you extend the exercise little by little. Eventually, your dog will be sitting down quietly until you command him to get up.

But now, you're entitled to assemble the equipment you need for your dog training.

Your Shopping List

Many of the things you need for training your dog you will possess already since you need them every day. My personal experience with these things has been good, and in my view that's more or less it. You don't need more stuff for educating your dog successfully. Actually, it's very handy that you can put these things in the pocket of your coat and train your dog very spontaneously when being outdoors.

- ❖ Collar

- ❖ Leash

- ❖ Dog whistle

- ❖ Clicker

- ❖ Treat

- ❖ Toy

Buying a collar, please make sure it fits well. Your dogs shouldn't be able to slip out of it with his head. But it shouldn't be too tight, either. Also, it should be adjustable in size and lockable. I don't like those collars that can be tightened because they strangle the dog whenever he outruns the length of the leash.

Personally, I prefer breast harnesses which have been in use ever since I had my first dog. Their advantage is that you dog won't hurt himself when pulling on the leash. If you want to do track work with your dog or you want him to learn not to pull on the leash, you can use a collar in addition. When training with him, just fix the leash on the collar. After your training you can re-attach it to the breast harness. Of course, you've got the option to work with two leashes. If the pull on the leash is too strong, you can let go the leash when to the collar and control your dog with his breast harness.

But when walking the dog as part of the daily routine, you can use a basic leash or a retractable leash. Using the basic leash, your dog is forced to move closer to you. A retractable leash, on the other hand, leaves him more moving space which you can restrict by pressing the stop button. The retractable leash is a great choice, in my view. When being in the city I can hold the leash short. As soon as we're somewhere out in a field, he can move freely within a radius of 5 meters. As far as your training is concerned, a towline is a good choice. It's got a length of 10 meters and more, and you can let you dog run off while still being in control. However, the towline proves inconvenient for the purpose of your daily walks because you have to hold quite a big pile of leash in your hand.

If you can't whistle, go for the dog whistle. It's a great tool for help. Just whistling once you signal your dog to come up to you. Well, it should be mentioned that first of all your dog has to learn to obey to the sound of the whistle. There are dog whistles in various shades of sound available. If happened to me that when I used the whistle a strange dog came up to me. His owner might have had the same type of whistle ...

Treats are a must, and you should always have them in your pocket. You have to reward your dog and by giving him a fine treat you can never lose. As you know you have to reduce the treat little by little. No doubt, if your dog is older, you can occasionally reward and spoil him with a treat when doing your round. If you can't have the treat in the pocket of your coat, you can use those convenient bags you can attach to the belt loop of your pants, so you can reach the treat very quickly. If you carry the treat in a plastic bag, for example, the moment of praise would often be gone before you can even unwrap it.

Apart from that, you should always have a toy on you, for example a throwing or pulling toy which gives you the chance for a spontaneous play in-between.

Now, you're ready to go shopping and assemble your equipment. If you're not so sure about the size of the dog harness, always go for one that is adjustable. If you like, you can take your dog with you. Most of the dog markets have no objections and admit dogs for fitting purposes.

But be choosy as to the quality of your equipment. It should be good because you want your stuff to remain functional for a long time. That applies to the leash in particular, since it will be used an awful lot in the beginning. Therefore, it's worth spending a bit more money on it. As far as harness and collar are concerned, I would go for a less expensive model because the little one will outgrow it soon.

To Adapt the Dog to New Impressions

As soon as your puppy has moved in, you have to make him get used to his new place of living. That means not only does he have to get to know his family and the apartment, but also is it necessary for him to get accustomed to all the noises around him and belonging to his daily life.

If you plan to take your dog downtown, you should plan city excursions with him. He can learn that the places are busy with many people. It would not bother him at that age. But when he's grown up, he might easily get nervous in situations he has never experienced before. Should you live on a noisy road, walk your puppy right there. He must get to know the sound of cars, and that can be very noisy.

When socializing your dog, focus on doing it in accordance with the needs of the species. A herding dog has needs that are different from those of a typical family dog. The herding dog might have to learn that a tractor is noisy and what sheep are. If you have a family dog, he must cope with considerably more impressions in his life.

The socialization of your dog should be well planned, and don't ask too much of the small dog. Go walk with him downtown for 15 minutes and grant him rest after that. Try to offer him a new impression every day. Since there are many stimuli downtown, your first excursions there should be at a time when the place is not too crowded with people. During your tour, please focus completely on your puppy. If he stays quiet and follows you obediently, he should get a treat, no question. Thus, you can make him learn that the city doesn't mean something negative for him. And if he gets a treat, that's only positive, isn't it?

But if you feel that your puppy is overstrained and gets nervous, finish your excursion and try it again the next day. In case of doubt, you can go on shorter tours with him around the city until you are sure he's become used to it. That's where your empathy comes in because no puppy reacts the same to stimuli from his surroundings.

There are puppies that aren't very fearful and reserved. In such a case the dog needs your motivation. Don't drag him after you and force him to do something. Try to persuade him kindly and lure him with a toy. Reward him for even the smallest success because the rascal must learn that everything is okay. It's you who makes him feel secure which, again, strengthens his bond of trust with you.

How to Build up a Good Relationship

Now we are on the next important subject: "Bonding". You're aware of the fact that if there is a strong bond between you and your dog, he will go through thick and thin with you and respects you as alpha animal of the pack. That's the most important building block of your relationship.

Usually, a puppy bonds easily to a person, since his instinct tells him that his own survival won't be possible without you. That's why you've got good chances that your puppy will build up a strong relationship with you. All mistakes you make in this phase can cause permanent damage. He might not have real trust in you and bonding might not work, either. It's very hard to direct your dog back on the right track again once his trust is damaged, and in some cases grown-up dogs won't respond to even your best of efforts. That's why you should keep an eye on how you deal with your puppy.

Be together with your dog as much as you can and show him that he can have a lot of playing fun with you, too. Bonding walks are highly recommendable, and you can have a lot of fun together. Take all the time you need. That's all-important for your future family life together.

The puppy still has the instinct to follow you. So, take him to a big meadow and make sure there are no cars in the around. Place him on the ground and walk a few steps. You might have to lure the little one at first, or he might follow you straight from the start. Then you should walk off in another direction. If you see that your dog will pass you or runs off into the opposite direction, change your direction immediately. These bonding walks contribute to the education of the puppy, since in order to not lose sight of you, he will have to learn to be attentive where you walk to.

You should go for such a bonding walk once every day, and it shouldn't take longer than 5 minutes. As soon as your dog is 16 weeks old, you can extend your exercise to 15 minutes. Make sure that you change the places you go and that there is no traffic around. Once your dog knows the terrain, it will become harder for you to make him follow you. Even when your dog has grown older, you can still make these bonding walks with him. And you can also choose a wooded area or rough terrain for your walks. We will come back to that subject later. But starting off with bonding, it's sufficient to use a big meadow for your exercises, so the puppy can learn to follow you and watch where you are.

Now, we're entering on a likewise important subject, since "manners" are the name of the game.

The Etiquette-Guide for Dogs

Did you ever wonder why certain people are afraid of dogs? Often, they have just made bad experiences with a four-legged friend. But I have no intention to blame that on the dog's paws - no, to the contrary, in most cases it's to be blamed on the owner. Certainly, you will have witnessed such a situation yourself. And, honestly, I sometimes really wonder what these people think they're up to.

Let me give you an example to clarify what I mean: One day, I went to the play yard with my kids. It was clearly signposted on the green parts of the yard that dogs are to be kept on a leash. Obviously, one dog-owner didn't care at all, his dog was running among the playing kids and even tried to chase them. He would jump up at them and even knock over one or two of them. I went up to the owner, asking if his own kid would be playing here on the meadow, too. He denied and commented wouldn't it be just great how his dog would be playing with the kids. As I said to him that dogs are to be kept on a leash in this yard and this would be a playground for kids, he just gave a shrug. On my reply that this would be quite a dangerous situation and that his dog would be working off his hunting instinct, he said laughing: "He just wants to play." These words I do hear very often, and then, all of a sudden, situations like that escalate. In the meantime, other parents had joined our debate, and one father finally called the police since the dog-owner just didn't want to show sense.

Unfortunately, such situations belong to daily routine. The dog-owner wasn't aware of the fact that his dog could have bitten somebody in the yard. All that mattered to him was that his dog could romp about at will, while he himself didn't have to move an inch.

That's the reason why I'm coming to the Etiquette for Dogs now, which your dog has to learn inside out. However, it's up to your responsibility as a dog-owner to teach him good habits in the first place. That also means that you have to adhere to certain rules.

What I personally consider highly important: Pick up the droppings of your dog, even if you don't feel comfortable doing it - it's simply rude to leave the droppings where they are, all the more it's simply environmental pollution. However, much more important is that you carry the bag in which you put the droppings to the nearest trash bin and refrain from deposing of it in nearby shrubs. Unfortunately, that's exactly what happens quite often. Along our own daily walking route, which is co-used by many dog-owners, the shrubs are littered with such bags. Why that?

But there is another point that is truly dear to me: Always take serious the fear other people or other dogs might have. Saying "He just wants to play" is no argument at all. Whenever you see a kid, an adult or a strange dog coming up and arousing interest in your dog, put him on the leash. Let him walk "at the heel" and prevent him from approaching the object of interest. Being on the leash, he can still play with other dogs. But first of all, check out if the strange dog and his owner agree.

You realize, it's simply about showing consideration for others.

So, what is the Etiquette for Dogs actually made of?

Teach your dog that he must not jump up to people. It's not only because his dirty paws soil the clothing, but a big dog can also easily knock you over when taking a running jump on you. You just can't imagine what can happen to a kid.

The dog jumps up on you because he wants to reach your face. It's his inborn nature to lick the muzzle of the higher-ranking animal, in this case it's you, when welcoming or appeasing him. But there are dogs that jump up on you because they simply seek your attention. Now, you've got two options to make your dog give up that behaviour:

First, ignore him. Then, should you see he intends to jump up on you, turn away from him. Turn back only if you see that he has given up his attempt. Alternatively, you can command him straight away. If he wants to jump up on you, command "Sit" and, should he stay in that position, praise him for complying. What counts here is your swiftness. If the dog is already galloping up at you with speed, it should be rather difficult to command him to sit.

Another point to be discussed is "begging": Some dogs are master beggars. Some of them just look at you with their big, beautiful eyes and watch closely every bit of food you take to your mouth, while others start barking to get your attention. "Hello, I'm sitting down here and would like to have something, too."

What you can do in such a case: Ignore your dog and don't look at him. He will soon realize that it is useless and will leave or lie down. However, that only works, if your dog's just looking and not barking or even sitting up and begging. Should your dog try to reach onto the table with his fore paws, put him on the leash, perhaps at a certain distance from the table, and keep on ignoring him. If you have finished your meal and if has been quiet in the meantime, he can get his deserved attention. Another possibility is to command the dog "Down" and "Stay". He must execute this command as long as you're sitting at the table having your meal. After the meal, you terminate the exercise by giving him a good amount of praise.

In no case, however, you must bar your dog from the room you're eating. You would prevent him from learning how to behave at table, which, consequently, will cause problems, for example, if you want to take him to a biergarten after your usual tour.

Please make sure that he won't get a treat from everybody else who come to see you. He will surely remember that and start begging everybody for treats. My Dachshund knew that he would get a treat from my mother whenever she came. As a matter of fact, she always had one on her. And if she forgot it, Bennie would literally hang on to her bag to burrow it through with his mouth. He thought there might be a treat for him somewhere inside. As far as my Chi was concerned, I forbid people who came to see me to bring treats. Well, he was happy getting this or that treat I had given to my visitors before, but it was never a big deal for him, if there was nothing. He was content being overwhelmed with tender loving care.

Another subject of great importance the Etiquette for Dogs deals with is "hunting": Every dog's got his hunting instinct - sometimes more, sometimes less intensive. Some dogs chase people who are jogging, riding on their bikes, or are just after everything that's moving fast. Stop it right away, or it will be a tedious job to correct that behaviour later. Don't forget that an untrained dog with strong hunting instincts must be kept on a leash. Otherwise, it can happen that his behaviour is more than just bothersome for bikers and joggers in the town park.

What is important is to keep your dog busy because he needs to work off somehow. Encourage him to burn off energy. You can make use of throwing games, but also of dog agility. A dog that's sufficiently encouraged, whose mind must be active and who gets enough exercise, has lost his keen interest in chasing things. Also, you should try to distract him with a toy. Take his favourite toy and as soon as you see that he starts focussing too much on the birds in the field, distract him with his toy.

Another important point here is "obedience". Train you dog as follows: If somebody is approaching on a bike, let your dog come up and sit down next to you by using the "Sit" command. Make sure that he's looking only at you. As soon as the biker is out of sight again and your dog has been keeping strict eye contact with you, he can get his praise and be commanded to get up again. However, if you see that your dog is unable to concentrate and that his glance is straying, you have to make him look back at you. You can achieve that by calling his name so that, immediately, he feels addressed and turns his eyes back to you.

During your obedience training it's important to keep the dog on the leash until he has learned how to behave right. For training purposes, you should pick trails and walks where you meet a lot of joggers or bikers who pass you by. In order to consolidate what your dog has learned, proceed as follows: If your dog enjoys retrieving, throw the toy, but don't let him run off after it right away. He should stay with you until you explicitly tell him to retrieve the toy.

Meeting other dogs is something he must learn as well. That's one subject, I must say, that is covered in the "Etiquette-Guide for Dogs" which doesn't work out very often and but leaves injured dogs.

If you meet a strange dog that is on the least while doing your round, put your dog on the leash, too, or at least, call him to come to you. Your dog might behave well, but you never know why the other dog was put on the leash in the first place. And the other way round: If you keep your dog on the leash and you meet a strange dog that is not on the leash, kindly ask the owner to call his dog to him.

Why?

There are reasons why a dog is being kept on the leash:

- ➢ The dog is in the process of learning.

- ➢ The dog is fearful, insecure or aggressive.

- ➢ The dog is in heat.

➤ The dog is sick.

So, you see there are several reasons which in fact require a dog to be kept on a leash, and you never know which is applicable.

Dogs that are usually kept on the leash, are not allowed to get in touch with other dogs or other people. Generally speaking, that's what I was taught at the dog school. And I can confirm that myself. When kept on the leash my Chi is quite aggressive, if another dog gets too close to him. But being not on the leash, he would behave relaxed.

The leash is restricting the room to move for a dog and there are dogs that appear to be aware of the fact that they can't run off to flee a fighting situation.

If your dog is not on the leash and you let him be with other dogs, you signal him in a way that he's allowed to pull on it. And he will certainly do that. In order to sniff at them he's eager to be with his kind as fast as possible.

Keeping the dog on the leash should mean for your dog walking obediently next to you and staying quiet. If you see that your dog is aggressive towards his fellow-dogs when on the leash, distract him as soon as you see a strange dog coming into sight.

Now, I'm coming to the subject "staying alone in the house". Well, this subject too has good potential to cause trouble, especially if you live in a rental apartment. Needless to say, your dog wants to be part of everything you do and that should be his intention. But sometimes it simply doesn't make sense. So, your dog must learn to stay alone at home for a few hours. We're not talking about your eight-hour working day. As mentioned before that's not the point. No dog should be left alone for eight hours a day.

Proceed slowly with your training to teach him to stay alone, so he can learn step by step and it won't be a shock for him, should you be out for several hours. Some dogs cope with it well, while others bark and yelp incessantly until their owner is back.

Proceed carefully and use the following exercise: Go into the bathroom and lock the door behind you. As soon as your dog begins to protest loudly, ignore him and leave the bathroom only if he's become quiet again. It that works, you proceed with your training, leave the apartment, close the door and stay outside for a few minutes. If your dog's become quiet again, you come back in. Extend this exercise step by step and up to 30 minutes. Your dog will learn that being alone isn't a bad thing at all and that you come back quite soon.

Please refrain from making a big deal about seeing your dog off or saying goodbye to him.

Your puppy shouldn't stay alone for more than a couple of minutes. His instinct to follow you is still very strong and present and he feels threatened when being alone. He's terrified and staying alone in the house will become a hard thing for him from the very beginning.

Needless to say, before staying alone your dog should have been outside to empty himself and, perhaps, had a chance to be romping about for a while. To keep him busy, give him a bone to chew while you're absent.

I recommend you not to grant your dog access to all rooms in the house when you start your training. A puppy or a teen dog can have stupid ideas when being alone. It's sufficient, if he can stay in the lobby, perhaps the kitchen or the living room. It's completely up to you which rooms make best sense for you.

Those were the principal points of the "Etiquette-Guide for Dogs" which I consider important for you to know. Needless to say, you can add whatever you deem necessary, but you will see that, ultimately, everything comes down to good education. It's a heartfelt concern of mine that you fully accept your responsibilities as a dog-owner and comply with the rules of the "Etiquette-Guide" for the sake of your fellow-humans.

Watch for the Needs of Species and Breed

Even if every dog should know the same basic commands, you have to bear in mind that the needs of your dog are to be considered well in everything you do. You can't demand of a herding dog to integrate like a well-behaved family member that is content with usual walks. A Jack Russell, for example, is a highly energetic animal that wants to romp about and really needs to do it. If you don't comply with your dog's natural needs, you can soon get in trouble.

There are dogs that get aggressive, if their needs are not met with. They tend to develop bad habits or destructiveness when being alone. It might happen that a dog that's bored eats all the time and just gains weight.

So, it's important for the well-being of your dog to be fully occupied, and he must be physically active, too. But don't forget the headwork. If you go for a hunting dog breed, the dog should be able to satisfy his hunting instincts. Work underload would be troublesome for the dog.

That's why you should definitely get as much information as possible about the dog species and breed you wish to have. And ask yourself if you can really cope with his natural needs. Do you have the time to go to the exercise ground with your dog and challenge him? Do you want to go for daily walks through woods or across fields for many hours? In every weather? Or do you prefer to have a typical family dog that enjoys playing around, but won't be used as a guardian dog?

Many questions, I know. But you have to think about these questions. It may sound strange, but going for the wrong breed, you will soon experience a great amount of frustration in your home. Our Dachshund-German Spitz mixed-breed was the outstanding example for a hunting dog. He enjoyed running through the woods and burrowing in holes, sometimes that deep that his entire head was gone inside the hole. Tracking was his natural gift, and so I would be in the woods with him for many hours, lay trails in our garden or while on our daily walk. He was just loving it because he was simply in need of that kind of challenge. My Chi, on the other hand, is a little hurricane that enjoys darting across meadows and can't be stopped by either small obstacles or wet weather. In summer we're out very often, whereas in wet and cold weather he's fully content with short walks and would even decide for himself when to head home again.

I for myself adore both breeds. However, I wasn't aware of the fact that a mixed-breed can have such distinct characteristics of a Dachshund. For which reason I had to learn to play my role and had to live with such and such bad habit my dog used to exhibit at home.

Apart from considering the right breed, you should also ascertain, if the dog is suitable for beginners or experienced dog owners. There are dog breeds that can be educated easily and are very teachable, while others need a more experienced owner and a stringent hand.

How to be a Good Team:
10 Tips to be Successful

Both you and your dog have to get to know each other well, and there's a lot of work ahead of you. But you're rewarded, becoming a great team. Below you find my 10 ultimate tips for achieving this goal:

1. Don't overstrain your dog

It's not you who determines the duration of your training sessions, it's your dog - well, at least indirectly. Adjust the exercises to his age and his ability to concentrate. Compared to a grown-up dog, a very young dog wouldn't be able to concentrate for very long. So have short breaks in-between the exercises and use them for playing with your dog. But always bear in mind that it's officially you who decides when a training session begins and when it ends. It's not your dog.

2. Correct your dog properly

It's not a bad thing at all to correct a dog but see that you correct him the moment you detect him doing something wrong. If you correct him too late, he wouldn't know anymore what you correct him for. An example: If your dog doesn't want to stay in the "Sit" position, correct him the moment he's willing to get up. If he's already up, he wouldn't probably know what he has done wrong.

3. You're important for him

It's great for a dog to be able to play around while you walk him. But also try to use your walks for short exercises in-between. Thus, your dog will learn that your walks are good fun for him, but also that it's his task to be watching out for you. Thus, he learns that he can have a lot of fun with you and not only with his fellow-dogs.

4. Use body language

You have to show your dog that you mean the things you tell him, and that's by using your body language. Dogs pay good attention to body language, and if you don't reinforce your "No" by shaking your head, your dog won't take your command seriously. The more important the matter you want to convey, the more energetic and resolute you have to be. Picture for a moment you're sitting cross-legged on a bench in a park, and you want to call your dog to come to you using the "Come" command. He will probably stay indifferent. But if you get up from the bench and give him the hint to come up to you, you clearly reinforce your command.

5. Change your routine

If your dog masters his training and knows an exercise inside out, let him do it again and afterwards change your routine. If you do the same exercise over and over again, your dog starts to get bored. Of course, it's always a good idea to repeat the exercises several times a day, but please be mindful of intervals.

6. The right communication

Your voice is as important as your body language. Its sound should always be in keeping with the meaning of your commands. For example, don't give the "No" command with a low and caressing voice, but chose a resolute and harsh sound, whereas you "Good Dog" should be nice and sweet again.

7. Train your dog properly

Training your dog, you have to watch closely to see if everything is done right. That's how you make sure your dog can put all those things he's being taught by you into proper practice. But should you negligently turn a blind eye to that, he will execute many commands without knowing why or only half-heartedly. That, however, can frustrate your dog, especially if certain commands are concerned.

8. Watch your moods

Train with your dog every day and on a regular basis. But avoid doing so, if you are stressed or edgy. Your moods are transferred onto the dog, yet he doesn't understand them which can spoil your educational success in the end.

9. Reward the dog properly

As mentioned above, there's not need to work with treats all the time. For example, you can pick a certain toy as a reward which your dog only gets, if he did something well. But take the toy away from him after your reward game because it should always be something special for your dog to play with.

10. Treats

If you want to reward your dog with a treat during an exercise, you should always go for small pieces and try to hold them in your hand. It's important that you give the treat right after your dog's done something well. If he gets the treat too late, he won't know what he gets it for, and likewise won't understand that he completed the exercise as expected.

I have been rather successful bearing these 10 points in mind. But let's be honest: Sometimes it simply doesn't work - if that happens, you need to continue with a twinkle in your eye. Dogs can have bad days, too, and can be unwilling to do something. As long as it doesn't become a rule, just let it happen and you can take a day off from the usual training routine.

But now let's come to the Training Schedule itself.

The 10x10 Training Schedule

Basic Training

Level 1

❖ *What's my name?*

It's very meaningful for your puppy to know his name. If he knows his name, he will react when addressed. So, start your training with teaching his name - immediately after the puppy has moved into your home. Make sure he's looking at you and say his name. It is advisable to say his name whenever you demand something of him. For example: "Bruno, this is your food" or "Bruno", come here". Everything that has to do with your dog, should be linked to his name.

It won't be long before your dog knows exactly that you mean him whenever you say his name. If your dog can be easily distracted or appears to be unwilling, try to bribe him with a treat. Say his name and as soon turns around to you give him a treat.

You dog will associate with the treat that it is good for him to react to this word you keep saying. But bear in mind that the name itself has no meaning for the dog. There are dogs like for example my Felix that would usually get attentive and look at me whatever I may say. Even if I just call the kids, the dog would be running along because he knows there might be something great for him he doesn't want to miss.

From the sound of your voice the dog will judge if it's worthwhile reacting to his name or not. If you're angry, you will express that mood in your voice. In such a case, you better refrain from calling your dog. Otherwise he would be anxious and have the uneasy feeling that he has done something wrong. Of course, you will occasionally call him when you're upset because he did something stupid. That's inevitable. But right at the beginning when he still has to learn to react to his name, he should connect your call with a positive kind of experience. If you call his name only when he was naughty, he won't be willing to react to his name and will always connect something bad with it.

❖ _Sit_

This is a basic command which is very important for the two of you. If you say it, you get your dog in the state of rest and prevent him from running to and from between your legs. Dog-owners like to use the "Sit" command before they start their exercises. The dog must sit down and pay full attention to what you do.

There are two ways to train the "Sit" command with your dog: Either actively in that you assist your dog in executing it, or indirectly in that you teach it out of his training action.

Should you choose the first possibility, you must hold a treat up high between the thumb and middle finger, while your index finger is pointing upwards. Then you move the treat past his muzzle and slowly upwards. Now for keeping his eye on the treat, the dog is forced to sit down. As soon as he sits, you say the "Sit" command and reward him with his treat.

Alternatively, you can apply some pressure on his bottom with your hand. When he sits, you say the command and he can have his treat.

There is a reason why your finger must be outstretched in this exercise. It signals your dog to sit down. My Dachshund, for example, was hard of hearing in his old age, but as a puppy he had learned the hand gestures that go together with the basic commands. So, he always knew what I wanted him to do. If the hand gestures are taught right at the beginning of your dog's education, it will be sufficient to call his name in later years. He will look at you, and all you will have to do is make the adequate hand gesture without saying a word.

As I mentioned before, you can also teach your dog commands out of the training action which, particularly, makes sense when the exercises for your dog have become more complex and more difficult. But for you, it means that you have to watch your dog always closely.

As soon as he sits down, you say the command while you give him his treat. Without much effort, you can teach him to execute "Sit" command. Trust me, you will have the opportunity to train that command several times, because your dog will sit down a lot of times during the day.

❖ _Down_

This basic command is equally important for a good and working cooperation with your dog. You can train the "Down" command directly or later in connection with the "Sit" command.

Take a treat and holding it between thumb and index finger put it in front of your dog's muzzle. Then move your hand upwards and over his head. In order to be able to keep an eye on his treat, he is forced to lie down and tilt his head further back. And now you could stretch out your other open hand downwards to teach your dog the right-hand gesture that goes with the command.

Should your dog decline to comply with your "Down" command, assist him. Let him take the "Sit" position first, and then carefully pull his fore paws forwards until he's lying down as you wish. Now you can say the right command and give him his treat.

But you can also train the "Down" command out of your training action. As soon as your dog is in the down position, command him and give him a treat. Again, it's worthwhile watching your dog closely during the day.

❖ *Go (with ball-throwing)*

A dog that's well-behaved should never run off without your explicit command. That's highly important for the time to come and, particularly, if you have got a big dog breed. You determine the moment he can run off. At the very start of your exercise, he will probably run off straight away as soon as you have thrown the ball. That's not a bad thing because he will learn to comply with your command.

You should train that in your private garden or in a fenced-in place, so your dog can't run away. There shouldn't be any cars around. To comply with your command, you have to put him off leash. If you use a towline, the exercise is only suitable to a certain extent, for which reason I wouldn't recommend it.

Demand attention of your dog in a way that he has to look at you and you can show him the ball. Then you throw it and the moment your dog runs off, you say "Go". Good timing is decisive here so the dog can really connect his running with your command.

In this case you don't need a treat since the ball you have thrown will be his reward to run after.

Let me add something about the towline at this point of my explanations: I'm aware that many dog-owners have no private garden to use for their dog training, so things become a bit more difficult for them. If you wish to train with a towline, pick one with a length of a few meters and don't throw the ball too far. Your puppy could hurt himself seriously when running at full speed after the ball and, all of a sudden, your line proves to be too short. Apart from that there is the real danger that your dog might get entangled. You have to put the entire loose line on the ground so it can't stop him. Well, I have to say that my mixed-breed always made it somehow to get the line between his legs. But I didn't want to run the risk of his breaking a leg. So, you should also be cautious when using a towline.

❖ *Shake*

This is a nice command which is something like a staple for many dog-owners. Let your dog "Sit" and hold out your hand to him. As soon as he has placed his paw into your hand, you say the command and he gets his treat.

Here you can take his paw and put it into your palm. Most dogs learn very quickly what things are about in this exercise, and usually after a few trials will do the exercise by themselves.

As a rule, you can say, if your dog has mastered this command, it's sufficient to hold out your hand to him. He will understand what you want and place his paw into your palm.

❖ *Going into the basket*

Your dog must learn where his place is. And that's the basket. It's his sleeping place, but also the place he always can withdraw to, if he wants to be on his own for a change. And it has to be respected by every member of your family. Your dog has no room for himself, all he's got is his basket and it should always be a place he can rely on: "This is my place of rest, here I can relax and doze off."

Don't forget to show your puppy where his basket is when he's moving into your home. And keep this place always tidy.

To make your dog go into his basket you can chose a special command which you personally like. We use to say: "Go to your place."

Train this behaviour in that you take your dog to his basket saying the command you have chosen. Alternatively, you can teach your dog out of your training action. If you see your dog is just about to go into his basket, say the command and give him a treat.

Remember that your dog must connect his basket with something positive. Don't send him into his basket when he's done something stupid or wrong. You would punish him, and in this case he wouldn't like to use the basket any longer and couldn't relax in it.

My husband used to command our Chi into his basket a lot of times after he had been romping like crazy through the room. However, as a consequence, the dog looked out for another sleeping place and chose the basket for dirty laundry. If he was rebuked because he had been barking by the garden fence, he would go straight into the living room and lie down in his basket. For him it was something like a "seat of repentance". But to make him use the basket as a sleeping place again I put it somewhere else and lined it with discarded laundry for some time. Lo and behold - he accepted it as the laundry basket and now he behaves well again and sleeps in his basket.

❖ *Clearing up toys*

This is an exercise that makes fun and takes some work out of your hands. Primarily, your dog is kept busy, and he must use his mind to its full capacity. I mentioned elsewhere that your dog should have only a few toys because if there are too many toys on the ground, he will mostly lose his interest. But if your dog has a basket full of toys and can access it freely, he will come to take them out one after another and your room will soon be littered with them.

Let your dog take up a toy from the ground and then hold the basket under it. Then you command "Drop" and your dog should release the toy, while you add saying "Clear up". When done well, you give him a treat.

If he has mastered that, you can optionally place the basket at a certain distance, and it's the dog's task to bring the toy to the basket. In the course of this exercise, you will notice that you don't need to use the "Drop" command anymore. Instead, you just say "Clear up" and your dog will know what he's supposed to do.

In order to make him search for his scattered toys, you can integrate into your exercise commands like "Where the ball?" or "Where's the teddy?" or whatever you may chose. He will know that he's supposed to go search for it. As soon as he's got it, you say "Clear up" commanding him to put it into the basket.

This exercise may challenge your patience a bit, but my mixed-breed mastered it fairly soon. My Chi, however, preferred to play with the toys instead of putting them back into the basket. Even today, this exercise doesn't work out with him very smoothly and reliably.

❖ *Where's the ball?*

Some dog breeds just love search games. Saying the name of the toy, your dog will learn which toy he's supposed to bring. It's a good idea to conceive of a short and easy name for every of your dog's toys.

Take his favourite toy, show it to him and then hide it behind your back. While you make the toy appear and disappear quickly, you say, for example, the command "Where's the ball?". Then you produce the toy from behind your back again. After a few trials he will have understood and probably search the toy behind your back. As soon as he does that, you give him a treat.

Having mastered this exercise, you can throw the ball while you say the command. He will start his search right away, bring the toy back to you or play with it.

❖ *Drop!*

You need to train this command, since your dog has to learn to release things he's got in his mouth. It's completely up to you which command you chose to that end.

I usually train it during a game. Take a pulling toy and play with your dog. Then, stop suddenly. As soon as your dog has released the pulling toy, you say your command and give him a treat.

It's necessary to repeat this exercise over and over again. He's got to know it inside out. Your dog must learn to drop things on your command.

There are dog-owners you train their dog to refrain from eating food lying on the ground. That worked out well in the case of my mixed-breed. But whenever he roamed through the bushes, he obviously thought I might not see what he's doing. Often, he would bring back trash which had been thrown away carelessly by some strollers and that smelled like something edible. Without repeating this exercise many times, he would have surely upset his stomach more than once. Right at the start of our training sessions, he even devoured a table napkin lying in the meadow. Though able to shout the command at him, he had swallowed it up already.

I don't know how your dog would behave in such a situation, but I know today that this command is really very important in order to save your dog from upsetting his stomach.

❖ *No!*

This is the right command, if your dog does something he's not supposed to do. It tells him to stop whatever action immediately. We use the "No" command whenever we want to tell our dog to stop barking. Chihuahuas enjoy talking and they do talk a lot which, generally speaking, doesn't bother me at all. But our dog barks incessantly when people are passing by behind our garden fence. And that's quite annoying, I can tell. Apart from that he enjoys barking at dogs that are much bigger than him which, in the past, put us in dangerous situations at times.

I vividly remember how once he barked at an Old German Shepherd dog that was passing us quietly. But when Felix started barking at him, he obviously annoyed the Shepherd dog that really put his back into it immediately and wanted to rush at Felix. At the other end of the leash there was an elderly gentleman who couldn't stand up to the sheer power of the Shepherd dog. I had no other alternative than to release Felix' leash and enable him to run away quickly. Felix was faster and the Shepherd dog didn't obviously feel like chasing that little dog after a while. Blessing in disguise! At the time it happened Felix was still a young dog and in the process of learning. Anyway, I could teach him the "No" command very quickly.

He's allowed to bark, of course. But he has to know when to stop it, and he must not bark at other dogs, if these dogs behave peacefully or show no interest.

If you want to teach your dog the "No" command for something he does, you will need some patience.

If your dog barks, distract him while you say "No" to him. Then give him his treat. I used to hold his muzzle shut with my hand for a short while I said "No". But be careful! Don't squeeze his muzzle, the dog must be able to breathe.

Always bear in mind that "No" is no general command and should always be used referring to a certain thing or matter. If you train this command with the objective to stop him to bark, he won't understand what you demand of him, even if he's jumping up on you and you're saying "No". Always remember that dogs don't understand our language. They only learn to understand the commands we teach them. He can't put two and two together, and that's why he doesn't know that "No" is a word used for all sorts of undesired things.

Level 2

❖ *Become housebroken*

This subject is a significant one. Some puppies are more or less housebroken when they move into their new homes, while others still have to learn it. That also applies to dogs you may get from an animal shelter. Some know what it means, others still have to be taught to be housebroken. Generally speaking, every dog instinctively knows that he must not spoil his place, and he will know to avoid it. Unfortunately, he will look for another place in the house to spoil instead.

Go out with your puppy as often as possible. Best you do it when he's just got up from his nap, after he was fed or as soon as you notice he's becoming restless and starting to sniff at the ground.

Take your dog to a meadow, put him on the ground and say whatever command you like. Our puppies got to know the "Wee-Wee" command when tinkling. Your dog learns that he can empty himself in this place, which he should do in any case.

Should your dog urinate or do his dump in your house every once in a while, wipe it off without further comment and don't call him down. Generally speaking, it's not advisable to tell him off for it because he will connect something negative with it. That means that he might not want to urinate on the meadow anymore and retain it instead. But if he can be a good dog and relieve himself there, you should praise him for that.

Having a puppy means you will have to go out during the night. For a span of two weeks, we took our Chi outside the house every three hours. And after that he slept at least all night or, in urgent cases, he made a noise to let us know.

You must be consistent here because a dog that has never learned to be housebroken won't stop to relieve himself inside the house, that is, preferably in a certain spot. Admittedly, even if it's not suitable for a dog, our Chi learned to urinate on a special tinkle mat in very urgent cases when he was still a puppy. That turned out to be quite practical because now that he's growing older, he's got an enlarged prostate gland and, generally speaking, the pressure on his bladder is much higher. During daytime he can't retain it for more than three hours, and so he makes use of the mat when we're not at home and can't take him out.

Well, I'm not requesting you to teach your dog the same. I just wanted to mention to you that it's possible to teach things like that to a dog. The mat was placed next to the litter tray for the cat, rightly considered by our dog as a place for wee-wee. Well, he doesn't use the cat's tray as such, but should it become unbearable for him empties himself next to it and straight on the mat. Apparently, he's got a bad conscience, since he would get out of our way when we've come back home. But we won't tell him off. He can't be blamed for not being able to bear it for so long. And me, I can easily dispose of the mat afterwards. When we're at home, he will make us know that he needs to get out for a tinkle. He would stand in front of the door inside the house and start whining. That's something we haven't taught him. It's just his own habit.

As far as habits of cleanliness are concerned, our Chi is a very good example: He would go for his tinkle in the garden, but if it comes to the big business, he wants to be walked. So, I think he considers the garden his own place and, of course, that mustn't be spoiled.

If you wish to walk your dog in a relaxed manner, he must learn to walk on the leash. Particularly, if you have a bigger dog, behaving on a leash is an important subject. As the story with the German Shepherd dog, I told above clearly shows, it's almost impossible to walk with a bigger dog that works against the least with all his power.

First and foremost, the puppy has to get used to harness and leash. I recommend a breast harness instead of a neck harness. It's much comfier to wear for the dog, and he doesn't run the risk to strangle himself with it. Go for a breast harness that's not too tight-fitted. But it shouldn't be too loose, either. It should be easy to put your fingers between the breast harness and your dog. Apart from that, the harness shouldn't rub under the arms and cause your dog's skin to go sore.

Put the harness on your puppy during the day, so he's got enough time to get used to it. If you carry him to his accustomed place for wee-wee, put him on the leash, which should be hanging loose between you and your dog. If he starts running around, follow him. But also lure him into your direction because in the beginning the puppy will follow you everywhere you go. Thus, he learns that there's nothing bad about a leash.

As soon as your puppy walks with you on the leash, it's time to start your training. He must learn that it's you who determines the direction as well as the speed. If he starts running too fast or pulling at the leash, stop and change direction or speed. So, the dog is forced to adjust to you.

Later he will learn that he must behave well and walk next to you. Then, it's time to teach the "Heel" command which I will explain later. This command is quite difficult to learn for dogs that can be easily distracted or scared. It requires you to be resolute and, also, takes some time to teach.

❖ *From Sit to Down*

If your dog is well-behaved, complies with your "Sit" command and also knows the "Down" command, you can connect both exercises. First, let him take the "Sit" position and then command him "Down". Such combined exercises pose a challenge for the dog because he doesn't expect the command, he knows to be followed by another one which he doesn't know.

❖ _Retrieve_

Throwing sticks is an exercise most dogs really are keen on. But hard luck if you throw the ball of the stick and your dog's running out of sight with it. That often happens with dogs that haven't been taught the "Retrieve" command. Though they bring back the ball or the stick, they do so only when they deem it appropriate. If your dog wants to play, he will return it because he wants you to throw it again. However, he might have left the ball or the stick somewhere and comes back to you without it.

Your own house is a good location for teaching your dog this exercise. Throw his favourite toy and every time he comes back to you with it, you say "Retrieve". Needless to say, he should know the "Drop" command by then. Upon returning the toy, you give him a treat.

You can also teach this command out of your training action because the dog will bring back his toy, if he wants you to keep on playing with him. Therefore, it's wise to make use of this behaviour in order to integrate retrieving into his daily routine.

❖ _Sit with paw_

Another nice exercise which can be easily combined with others. If your dog has mastered the "Sit" and "Paw" commands, you can let him perform both. First, he must be sitting, then give paw. Perhaps you teach him to give paws by turns.

❖ *Going into the basket and staying there*

Your dog knows his basket already, and he also knows the command telling him to go there. Now, he still has to learn to stay there.

Send your dog to his place and command him "Sit" or "Down". Then you say "Stay" and wait a few seconds. A few seconds are enough in the beginning. When he's done everything as expected, you give him a treat and suspend your command by saying "Go". That means for the dog, he can get up again and change his position.

Keep on extending your "Stay" exercise and correct your dog in case he should finish it earlier. But never forget to finish an exercise. If you don't do that explicitly, your dog will get up at will which, however, means that training your dog will become very difficult. He will finish exercises whenever he deems it appropriate.

As soon as your dog knows to execute the "Stay" command, you can continue your dog-training on the meadow. Let him execute "Sit" and "Stay" and move a bit away from him while the dog must remain in the "Sit" position and must not run after you. Then you say the "Go" command which means for the dog that he can come up to you now.

It's important for your dog to learn the "Stay" command, even if it's not easy for lively dogs to master it completely. But what is the point in teaching all those basic commands, if you've got a dog that gets up too quick? That's why you must stay on the ball.

❖ *Intensify your training of clearing up toys*

You already taught your dog how to clear up toys. Now intensify your training. Leave the toy basket where it is and command your dog to bring his toys to it

If he's unwilling to comply, sit down next to the basket while holding a treat in your hand. He will now have a reason to come to you. Alternatively, you can say the names of the individual toys and let your dog bring these things separately.

I know a dog that loves to take care of clearing up things himself when he's given the command to do so. Well, you probably can't ask that of every dog. That's for sure. My Chi usually clears up the things you name and neglects the other toys lying on the ground. But perhaps that dog I just mentioned above is a kind of incentive for you to step up the training with your dog.

❖ *Calling your dog in your house*

Before your dog is allowed to run around with no leash outside your house, he must learn to come to you on your explicit call. As I said before, puppies still do that for a while entirely by natural instinct, but sooner or later the big wide world outside will be more interesting to him than you, and he will start roaming on his own, unless you hold him back.

So, leave the room you're just in and go into another room. Then call your dog's name together with the "Come" command. He will come up because he connects something good with the name and is hoping for a treat. If that works well in your house, you can train the same exercise with a towline outside. Give him a bit more of the leash and let him run freely. Then you call him. If everything works out as planned, your dog must stop for a second and come back to you.

Only if that works perfectly for both of you, and only if it really does, you can let your dog off leash. But you have to rely on him and that he will come back to you when you call him.

❖ *Drop and releasing the toy*

I told about that command further above. If you use the "Drop" command for something else, conceive of another command which is adequate.

Best use his favourite toy when playing with your dog. Most dogs won't like to release it. In your other hand you're holding a treat which you show your dog. As soon as the dog releases the toy, say the command you chose and give him the treat.

❖ *Intensify No*

That's something you need a lot of exercise for. As soon as your dog enters his teen age, he will ignore you or pretend not to be hearing your voice now and then. But "No" is a command of interdiction and, as a matter of fact, it must go smoothly.

Keep on repeating your training, and if your dog shows the slightest move to do a stupid thing, forbid him to do so immediately. But don't wait too long before things become completely uncontrollable. Command him to stop right away.

This exercise might not work on certain days. Then you have to change your strategy and distract your dog to prompt him to stop. For example, you can try another exercise. But always bear in mind that the distraction you chose is not considered a reward for your dog, like for example a ball game. That would make your dog ignore the "No" command categorically because he thinks he will get something superb from you.

Level 3

❖ *Look*

Off we go! Now you're elevating your training level considerably. In the meantime, your dog has learned hard mind work and how to cooperate with you. The "Look" command is about impulse control, which is of pivotal significance for dogs. Your dog must learn not to give in to his natural impulses. Practically speaking, that means, for example, that he mustn't chase the hare even if he's burning to do so. Instead, he must fully concentrate on you.

This exercise is a very difficult one for many dogs, since they would rather watch other things going on around than focus their glance on you. To be successful, proceed as follows:

Take a treat and hold it in your hand. Then command your dog "Sit" in front of you. Well, alternatively, he can sit down, if he likes to, or simply remain standing. That's completely up to you. Now you extend your arms to your dog. He will probably fix his eyes on your hands because he knows that you've got a treat he wants to have. As soon as he's looking at you and, I tell you, that will happen in no time, say the command and give him his treat.

You may wonder why I'm so certain that he will be looking at you? Because he's waiting for his treat, and if nothing happens, he will look at you with questioning eyes. Where is my treat? If that happens, you've reached the expected point in your exercise. Train that several times in a row and repeat the exercise as often as possible. This exercise helps you control your dog when he seems lost to all sorts of distractions on your walks.

I will explain later on how you can make his command more difficult for your dog.

❖ *Extending "Down" and "Stay"*

Not only are "Sit" and "Stay" important commands for your dog to learn, but also the "Down command is highly significant. If you command your dog to lie "Down" under the biergarten table, for example, you tell him to stay there, so other customers can't stumble over him.

You proceed here as you did with your "Sit" and "Stay" commands. Command your dog "Down", and then he must stay in this position for a certain span of time. If he knows the "Stay" command already, he won't be having much difficulty with that. Extend the time of your exercise step by step and, above all, stay quiet when correcting him for lying down in a different manner or for his willingness to get up again.

But don't eventually forget to resolve the exercise again. Never allow your dog to stay in the "Down" or "Stay" position and just go away. He will likely get up at will himself and your training effects would be spoiled.

❖ *Sitting up and begging*

People like to train that if they have a small dog. But big dogs won't fail, either. All that counts here is that your dog is not suffering from back and joint problems. Otherwise, you may overstrain him.

Take a treat between your fingers and show it to him. Now move your arm that's holding the treat higher and higher. Of course, the dog wants to reach the treat and so he will stretch his back until he's standing on his hind paws. Then you say the command "Sit up and Beg" and give him his treat.

This is a command dogs with short legs have difficulties to execute, for which reason you shouldn't overdo your training. If you have an older dog, you better leave it out since his back could cause him problems and he could feel pain afterwards.

❖ *Rolling*

Above all, kids have great fun with this exercise. You can train it actively and show your dog what to do. Or you train it out of your daily routine.

The easiest method is to watch your dog first, and the moment when he rolls onto his back and to the side, you say "Roll" and give him a treat. If you keep repeating that, he will know what this exercise is about fairly soon.

Some dogs like to roll on their backs, if they want to get belly scratches. In such a case, it will be rather difficult to train this command out of the action. So, he must show him in detail what he's supposed to do.

Command your dog "Down" and take a treat between your fingers so he can clearly see it. Now you move it away from his muzzle and sideways across his back. But do it very slowly so he is bound to turn around to follow it with his eyes. As soon as he can't turn his head any further and if he really wants the treat, he will have to turn around with his whole body. This is the exact moment you can give him his treat.

However, there are clever dogs that turn the head into the opposite direction because they know that their treat will have to appear on the other side. If that happens, it's important to wait at your dog's back so he will have a reason to turn his head into that direction. In case of doubt, you can also be of some assistance and push his body a bit when he's lying on his side.

But you shouldn't try this exercise when your dog is suffering from back or joint problems. And if your dog is older, please do it very carefully. Dogs with short legs and a long back encounter difficulties trying to execute this exercise and are more reminiscent of a fish on dry land than anything else, like in the case of my mixed-breed way back when. As a Dachshund-German Spitz mixed-breed and having the body form of a Dachshund he had trouble doing it. That's why I refrained from extending this exercise with him.

❖ *Bowing down*

Isn't it nice if a dog is making a bow in front of you? You can use this exercise later in the context of Dog-Dancing.

Let the dog be standing in front of you and show him his treat. Now, you move it from his muzzle to the ground and away from the dog. Your dog will stretch his body to reach it and will have to bow down. As soon as he's down and his rear shows upward, you say the command and give him his treat.

You can train that behaviour out of action, so wait until your dog is stretching his body, say the command and give him a treat. A bow is something a dog makes several times a day, that is, when he's getting up. So, all you have to do is wait and see.

❖ *Understanding commands by means of hand signs*

Hand signs are practical. They enable you to communicate with your dog without words. I taught those signs to my first dog, and he could at least understand the basic commands when he had become hard of hearing.

You can best train hand signs when teaching your dog a spoken command. Use the right-hand sign with every command, however, you have to make sure your dog is looking at you and can watch you making the sign.

There will be no appropriate hand signs for a number of commands. So, think carefully which exercises you want to do make without the use of words. Or you can use a target stick. How you train with it, will be explained to you later on.

If you want your dog to respond to hand sign commands only, you have to make sure he's looking at you and pays full attention to what you're doing. For example, you won't get an overexcited dog to sit down by using a hand sign. It will simply escape his attention, and he will need to hear your voice to respond.

Train hand signs with your dog on a regular basis, so he won't forget them again.

❖ *Giving paw by turns*

If your dog has learned to give one paw, you can also teach him to give paws by turns.

Either you hold out your right hand to him for his left paw or your left hand for his right paw. Or you teach him to give you the right paw on your command. Giving you the right paw, you say the "Right Paw" command and give him a treat, if he did it well.

Giving paws by turns you can facilitate by using the target stick. Tap his right paw with the stick and then tap the palm of your hand. If your dog knows how to give paw, it shouldn't be difficult for him to understand and to teach him giving paws by turns.

❖ *Clicker training or target stick*

Many dog-owners enjoy the clicker training, and the target stick is an ideal tool for working in the dog training ground, but also for dog-dancing or, simply, for all sorts of exercises.

But let's have a look at the differences and start off with the clicker training, more details of which you will learn later in this book.

For your dog, the clicker is a reward signal tool. Hearing its sound, he knows that he's been making his exercise successfully. That's why you have to make your dog get used to the clicker first, so he can connect something positive with the sound. Working with this tool, you can save yourself many treats which, by the way, is better for your dog's health.

The target stick is a tool to indicate to your dog the right direction or show him what to do. For example, is your dog supposed to move over a seesaw, you use the tip of the target stick to indicate to him the direction. Then you pull the tool along in front of your dog so he can follow it. Later on, during your training it's sufficient to put the target stick where your dog's supposed to move to. If you want him to put his paw into your hand, for example, first tap with it on his paw and then on your palm.

I recommend you focus on the subject "target stick" as best as possible. There are interesting books out dealing with it. For example, you may also learn how to use the target stick for dog-dancing in a very effective way.

I for myself do only have the clicker for practical training use, but I've read a lot about the target stick. Actually, I

like both tools, though personally I haven't had any use
for a target stick so far.

❖ *Clearing up toys on command*

Let's intensify the subject "clearing up". You can do that, if everything works well so far. Your dog knows the names of his toys by now and where they belong to. Why not try to animate him to clear up his toys without help?

Say the command "Clear up" when he's got a toy in his mouth already. If he brings you another one, you simply repeat the command.

You can as well tap on the toy with the target stick while commanding "Clear Up". In any case your dog must get the toy in question and put it into the basket. Instead of the target stick you can certainly use your fingers to indicate the toy.

Should your dog be a real work animal, he will greatly enjoy complying with the task and might even collect other things lying on the ground as well. The terrier of an acquaintance of mine had so much fun doing this exercise that he would clear up everything scattered on the ground in no time, also the toys of the kids. Everything landed in his basket.

My Chi, on the other hand, prefers precise instructions and therefore pauses after every toy to wait which one I command him to clear up next. Try to collect all toys in one big pile, so it might be easier for your dog to start off clearing up everything at once.

❖ *Naming toys and the dog must recognize the names*

I advised you before in this book to name all of your dog's toys. If your dog knows the names of the different toys, you can scatter several of them across the floor without a problem. Then you say to your dog "Ball" or "Stick" or whatever he's just busy with, and he must bring you the toy you named.

This exercise is suitable for mental work training because it means really hard-working time for your dog. If you prefer to make it a bit more complicated, just put more toys on the ground. You can even use other things that don't belong to your dog. In order to be successful, he will have to think hard and look for the right things.

Level 4

❖ *Call-back*

The call back is a command your dog must know inside out. As soon as your dog can walk with you off leash and there is no problem letting him play around on a meadow, you have to be sure that he's coming back to you straight away. Even if you throw a ball for him - as soon as you give the call back command, it's his task to ignore the ball and turn around to you immediately.

This exercise is a very important one for dogs with a strong hunting instinct that will have some difficulty in mastering it. When your dog is into his hunting mood, he can hardly stop himself, and that's exactly what needs to be trained.

Think of a word or phrase for your call back command. I use "Come here". Take his absolute favourite treat, so it's easier for you to tempt him back to you. In the beginning of your call-back training, I would go for the towline. My mixed-breed was like deaf when he got the smell of a rabbit in the woods or on a meadow. But nothing whatsoever could have ever distracted him once he was fully concentrated on the rabbit track. That's why I trained this command with a towline.

You can give your dog a treat in advance, so he knows you've got something delicious on you. Then, let him off leash and as soon as he's run far enough, try your call-back command holding the treat in his direction. Watch his positive body language. If your dog's coming up to you, he gets his treat. Using a towline, you can always pull him back into your direction should be unwilling to comply with the call-back command.

If you have the opportunity, do this exercise in a place where your dog can't just run away, like in your garden or on a fenced-in dog training ground.

❖ _Down and Stay for a while_

Now, it's time to extend your "Down" and "Stay" exercises further. Your goal should be to make your dog stay down until the exercise is resolved.

That's why you should take more time for practising that, which means let your dog remain in the "Down" position as long as you deem it appropriate, and you command him to get up again. Well, people say it's up to the dog-owner to correct his dog as soon as he's leaving the "Down" position and moving sideways. I take the view, however, that your dog should well have the opportunity to lay down comfortably, if you command him to remain in that position for an hour or even longer. The only thing he must comply with is the "Stay" command.

Training the "Down" and "Stay" commands with your dog you have to make up your mind if you really want to let your dog remain in the "Down" position for hours or if you allow him to lie down as comfortably as he can without any corrections on your part.

People sometimes forget to resolve this exercise which could cause some problems. Always remember, your obedient dog is behaving so well only because you demand it of him. So, finish the exercise in any case and don't just leave the house or the room without doing it. As mentioned elsewhere, your dog might then resolve it by himself which should be avoided. It's you who makes the decisions - not your dog!

❖ _Looking with toy in hand_

If your dog knows the "Look" command, you can make it more complicated by distracting him with his toys. That's, for example, a good option in case your dog's not overly interested in treats. Again, the main focus of this exercise is impulse control.

First, command your dog "Sit" or "Down". Pick a toy and hold it in your outstretched arm so your dog can clearly see it. Then throw the toy in the air and catch it again. It's important that your dog stays in his commanded position and won't try to catch the toy himself. If he does it right, give him a good praise.

This exercise is very hard to accomplish for the dog because he wants the toy so badly. Lively dogs in particular encounter problems doing this exercise. It's harder for them to control their natural impulses.

❖ _Running through pylons with help of target stick_

This exercise is a superb one, if you intend to train your dog in the dog-training ground. It's furthering his brainwork and, besides, it serves as a first dog-dancing session. As you see, this exercise is highly purposeful, once your dog knows it inside out.

The target stick tool should be known to your dog by now, and he should also know that there is nothing negative about that tool. He must also know how to follow the target stick. Let's proceed from the assumption that you have taught your dog these things already. Alternatively, you can use your fingers and a treat as pointers instead of target sticks.

Take your dog, advance with him to the first pylon and make sure he's standing next to you. Then, take a treat, hold it between your fingers, show it to him and, together with him, proceed through the first pylon. Your dog will be following you, if he wants to get the treat. With every pylon passed, he can get his treat.

When using a target stick, you dog should also be standing next to the pylon. Take the stick and tap between the two pylons, so your dog will follow your steps. As soon as he's left both pylons again, you give him his treat. That's how you proceed with the other pylons.

In case of doubt, you can take your dog by the collar and pass through the pylons together with him. A pylon done; your dog gets his reward.

It's important for you not to ask too much of your dog in this exercise. In the beginning, of course, it won't come to him naturally to pass through the pylons. Instead, and very often he will just pass them by. Always stay on the ball! He will soon know how to do it properly.

❖ *Putting paw on stool*

This is a very good modular exercise in connection with your "Give Paw!" command. If your dog is a master at that already, you just swap your hand for a stool. You can start off-putting your hand on a stool while the back of it is facing up. Your dog will understand that and, on your command, put his paw into your hand, just as he has learned.

After a few trials you can proceed and try it without using your hand. Think of a short command. The longer it is, the less your dog will be able to understand it.

❖ *Putting head on stool*

This exercise requires a little more time again, though some dogs may get it quickly. The goal is to teach your dog to put his head, that is his chin, on a stool.

You can facilitate this exercise by taking a stool with the appropriate height. If your dog complies with the "Down" command and is stretching his head forward, the stool should be fitting under his chin.

Command the dog to lie down and position the stool in front of him. Then, take a treat, hold it out to him and move it across the stool and back to you. You dog mustn't move, but he will follow the treat with his head. As soon as his head is positioned over the stool and his chin respectively his neck is touching it, praise him for that and give him his treat. Optionally, you can push his head smoothly down so it can rest on the stool. Praise your dog immediately to make sure he knows what you praise him for.

For example, I could teach this exercise to my Chi out of our usual training action. When lying down, he would like to put his head on a cushion. Whenever he did that, I said the "Put Down" command and gave him his treat. We started off trying that exercise with a small footstool, and he put down his head on it quite naturally. So, it's worth while watching your dog. As said, some commands can best be taught out of the daily routine action and don't need much effort.

❖ _Shaking himself_

This exercise is almost an automatism, and it is great to be made out of action, too. Whenever your dog is shaking himself, you shout the command at him and give him a treat. Your dog would shake himself several times a day, so you've got the chance to train that behaviour very often.

But make sure you don't do this exercise with dogs that have back issues. My Chi, 10 years old by now, is having problems with his intervertebral discs. When his back's hurting, he can't even shake the rain out of his fur. Therefore, you should exercise "Shaking" only, if your dog's got a healthy back.

❖ *<u>Scratching himself</u>*

Another exercise easy to be accomplished out of action. You have the choice to train that in a rather general manner or with your special focus on certain body parts. If your dog starts scratching himself, say the command and give him a treat. Scratching itself is a kind of reward for him because it provides him a certain relief. That's why you can be sure he will learn this exercise fairly quickly.

❖ *Where's the foot?*

Having taught your dog this exercise, you have the option to extend it later as you please. For example, you could command your dog to get you your home slippers.

Show him your foot and command him to use his mouth to tap on your foot. Optionally, you can hold a treat to your foot. As soon as your dog touches it with his mouth, you say the command and give him his treat.

If you like, you can train this command with the target stick as well, so you may not have to bend forward several times.

❖ *Kissing*

Well, it's completely up to you if you wish to teach your dog this behaviour. Some owners don't like their dogs licking their face.

In most cases, however, it's very easy. Say the "Sit" command and move your cheeks closely to his mouth. Pow! - and most four-legged friends are licking with pleasure. If that happens, you've got your dog where you want him and can say the command.

Alternatively, you take a treat and move it from his mouth to your cheeks. If he touches your cheeks with his mouth, you say the command and reward him with a treat.

When giving a kiss, your dog doesn't necessarily have to lick over your entire face. It's enough, if he gives you a nudge.

Caution! If you chose the first variant, please make sure you're holding your cheeks to your dog only and not the front of your face. Automatically, you would stare him into the eyes, something which many dogs consider to be a threatening gesture. It would make him insecure and, surely, he wouldn't find the exercise great anymore.

Level 5

❖ *Staying alone*

Especially for young dogs, staying home alone is very difficult. He's not yet used to it and, so far, has been together with his mother or his sisters all the time. If you don't show patience here and, for example, suddenly leave your dog alone for a longer while, you might cause terrible fears of loss in him. From then on, he will be yelping, barking or doing stupid things when you're going out.

My advice is: Take all the time you need when your dog's moving in. Make sure your fridge is filled up, so you've got enough time to concentrate on him for the next days. You can move freely in your house and the little one will probably follow you everywhere you go. Unless it should also be ok with you because he will realize that you're coming back again.

If that works well, leave the room and lock the door behind you. If the little one starts barking, open the door again, so he can see you. If he stays quiet because he will hear you behind the door, leave it closed for a while.

If your puppy has mastered this obstacle, too, proceed, for example, with bringing out the trash. He might be waiting in front of the door of your house but will know for sure that you're back again in a few minutes' time. Now, you've got the chance to extend these periods and stay away for, say, 10 minutes. Eventually, you can leave your dog alone for 30 minutes without problems.

Make sure you've been out with your dog before you leave home and that he's had the opportunity to romp about. As a rule, he would be tired after that and will be having his nap. So, you can be sure the time you're out won't appear so long to him.

❖ *Down with roll*

To train this behaviour you command your dog to lie down. Perhaps he knows the "Roll" command already because it was part of your earlier training schedule. Now you combine two commands, something which poses another challenge for your dog.

When lying on the ground, you say the "Roll" command. If he knows how to make the roll, he will probably comply with your command without hesitation. Unless you teach him the roll.

You find instructions how you go about properly or out of action further above. Combined exercises make a change in the daily training routine, and you make sure that your dog won't lose the fun. Apart from that, more mind work is required to find out what exactly you want of him.

❖ *Look with distractions*

This exercise adds another level of difficulty to the "Look" command. Now, your dog must really behave while you demand a lot of him. But, in the end, he will succeed.

Command him to take a position you want, that is "Sit", "Down" or "Stand". Then, move a few meters away from him and put his favourite toy on the ground. Your dog would probably love to go and get it right away, but he must wait until you gave him the command to do so.

Only if standing next to him, you let him go to get his toy and, of course, to retrieve it, as well. You've got the option to reward him by letting him play as he likes.

If your dog runs off to get the toy without waiting for your command, take the toy off the ground again and start the exercise again.

❖ *Naming toy, dog must retrieve or clear up*

If your dog knows how to clear up, he will have learned to differentiate the words for his toys. So, it's time to step up the mental challenge.

Pile up all of his toys or scatter them on the ground. Then, name a toy and your dog is supposed to look for it. If done right, let him take the toy to his toy basket.

The best method to proceed is to command your dog to retrieve the toy first and praise him for that. Then, you return the toy to him and command him the way you've taught him to put it back into his toy basket.

If you've got the feeling that your dog is a little overstrained, try this exercise again with fewer toys. Some dogs can't cope with the sensory overload and start retrieving all sorts of things except for that you wanted them to retrieve.

As soon as he sees too many toys lying on the ground, my Chi literally goes berserk. Everything is tested and played with, and in the end, he's so out of his mind that he would retrieve his favourite toys to me but ignore the other things instead. Whereas, if I reduce the amount to three or four pieces, it usually works out quite well.

Please avoid putting your dog's favourite toys on the ground during the training. If he sees them, you can be sure he will be much more in the playing mood than focussing on your training.

❖ *Running through pylons, on call*

If your dog already knows what he has to do with the pylons and your training goes well, you can send him off on his own. But command him to "Sit" behind every pylon and move to the other end of it yourself.

Now you release your dog so he can run through the pylons. You won't have to explain it to him, since you showed him the direction in a previous exercise.

This is a great training, particularly if you plan to participate in dog sport events at a later time. You will have to cheer your dog on because he will have to be working through the obstacles by himself.

Of course, both of you can walk together through the pylons prior to the actual exercise in order to make sure your dog knows his way.

❖ *Standing on a stool with the forelegs*

Little feats are no problem for your dog. In this exercise it's time for the stool again. Your dog knows by now how to put a paw on the stool, but now you raise the level of the exercise by teaching him to put both paws on the stool.

You command him to "Sit" in front of the stool and start off with one paw. Having put it on the stool, you first tip his other paw and then the stool. As soon as your dog's put it on the stool, too, you say the command and reward him.

If that doesn't work so well, you can take his paw and put it on the stool yourself while saying the command.

If you dog is standing or sitting during this exercise, should depend on his body size and the height of the stool you use for it. With a big dog it probably doesn't matter. But should you have a small dog, there is sometimes no other choice for him but to remain standing.

That's something, by the way, you can include in your exercise. Let him sit and stand in front of the stool by turns. Thus, you keep on changing the exercise and it won't get boring for your dog. He will never know what comes next.

❖ _Extend walking at heel, with changing speed_

Walking at heel with your dog is something you will have to train over and over again, and you will have to correct him very often. When he's getting the smell of something great or just wants to sniff, he might suddenly fall behind and move more slowly or even faster than before.

Correct him whenever necessary - and if it doesn't work, determine the speed yourself. If your dog gets faster and faster, and you're at a loss to correct him, walk more slowly. Needless to say, you have to restrict the amount of leash you allow him to use. Alternatively, just change the walking direction and walk slightly to the right or slightly to the left. Your dog must follow you in any case. Don't forget to say the "Heel" command when he's moving well-behaved next to you and keeping up with your changing speed.

As mentioned before, this command is essential, should you have a big dog. Otherwise, you will encounter some difficulty holding him fast while he's bracing himself against the leash and wants to go sniffing instead of walking next to you.

But don't extend the training time over the complete walk but give your dog the chance to sniff at a corner here and there. Let your dog satisfy his basic needs while walking him. And that means he should also have time to read the news in the "dogs' newspaper" at the next three trees along your route.

❖ _Retrieving toys out of the water_

Is your dog a water lover? If yes, you can make your daily walks even more interesting for the two of you. Throw a toy into the water and let him retrieve it. Well, that's basically like the standard exercise on a meadow, the only difference being your dog needs to jump into the water.

If you've got a dog that's averse to water, you may take the chance to make him get used to it. If he loves to play throwing games, just throw his favourite toy - but don't throw it too far, it should stay close to the bank of the river or the lake or remain in shallow water. If the water is shallow, your dog will have to enter the water with his paws only. If it works well with him, you can throw his toy a bit farther away from the bank, so he will have to jump into the water with his whole body.

But don't forget that many bathing lakes are off limits for dogs in summer or during the bathing season. Also, make sure that the currents in the lake or in the river aren't too strong. Otherwise, your dog might be at the risk of being drifted off from the bank.

In the cold season of the year, you should always have a bathing towel with you when you're out with him. So, you can rub him dry immediately after the swimming and he won't catch a cold. Being in your car you can additionally wrap him up in a warm blanket.

Swimming is a good exercise for his joints and contributes to the strengthening of his muscles without much effort. Most big dogs love water, whereas the smaller breeds are generally not so fond of it.

My mixed-breed was a water lover, while my Chi rather prefers watching it from a distance. He won't even take his paws to the water. If your dog doesn't want that, it's not a bad thing at all. So please don't force him to go into the water. Splashing about in the water is cooling him off in the summer, but it's no big deal for me, if he refrains from doing that.

❖ *Intercepting a toy in mid-air*

Have you ever watched that on a meadow? It's astonishing how high some dogs can jump to fetch up their toy. Well, of course, small dogs are somehow left with nothing, though they might be able to jump up quite high as well.

This exercise is not suitable for dogs with joint or back issues. Even dogs with very short legs and a long back shouldn't be challenged that much.

The best thing you can do is use a disc for this exercise. It can be fetched up more easily while in mid-air. Say the "Stay" command and move away from your dog. Then, throw the disc and release him. Be sure, he won't waste any time to try to intercept the disc, since it stays much longer in mid-air than a ball usually does.

But if your dog doesn't want to do that, it's not a big deal at all. As said, not every dog likes this kind of game.

❖ _Using the mouth for tipping on a shoe_

By now, your dog is familiar with your foot. Now try out a shoe. Starting off you can still have the shoe on. Later on, you could also tell your dog to retrieve your shoe.

Use your finger or the target stick to tip on the shoe. If your dog understands, he will copy your behaviour. Alternatively, take a treat and move it to your shoe. As soon as your dog is tipping with his mouth on the shoe, say the command and give him his treat.

It's very important here that the shoe is contained in the command, so the dog can know what a shoe is and retrieve it later. I chose the word "Shoe" for the command. It's short and crisp and the dog has learned it quickly. On my command he would also retrieve shoes that are in lobby.

Caution! There are puppies that understand this exercise as an invitation to free nibbling and would nibble at all of your shoes afterwards. As soon as you see your dog starts chewing at the shoe with his teeth, finish the exercise immediately and command him to stop. He must learn to touch the shoe only with his mouth, but never with his teeth.

Leisure Time Training

Level 6

❖ *Sitting up and beg and moving a few steps on two legs*

You can also use this exercise for later dog-dancing sessions. But always bear in mind that it's difficult for the dog to walk on two legs. As I explained to you in the previous exercise, sitting up and beg is quite something to accomplish for a dog, depending on his body stature.

Let your dog sit up and beg, but you don't reward him with a treat right after that but move it a bit a closer to you. Your dog will follow the treat and run after it. A few steps walking on two legs won't pose a problem for the dog, and you can extend this exercise to more steps at a time.

But keep your training units simple and short, and refrain from repeating your training several times. As said before, this exercise is physically demanding for the back and joints, and some dogs simply have difficulties balancing out their body on their short legs.

Generally speaking, if you have a sly dog, you might get a problem, too. Our dog, for example, thought he might get something off the table when sitting up and beg and walking after me. He really tried to beg this way. You must ignore that at any rate! If you give in and give him praise, he feels but confirmed in his behaviour. You should praise him only if you have explicitly commanded him to do this exercise.

❖ *Jumping through a tire*

In any case, your dog should know how to do this exercise when being in the dog training ground or when attending a dog sport event. It's not hard for the dog to comply with, unless the tire in use is not too high. However, some dogs simply don't dare to jump through a tire.

So, it's wise to make sure your dog gets to know the tire prior to your exercise. To that end, place it on the ground so he can have the chance to sniff at it. Then, you put a treat in its middle. Your dog must tread on the tire to reach it and thus learns that there's nothing dangerous about it.

After that, you position the tire upright but make sure it's still touching the ground. Put the treat on the other side of the tire and then let your dog move through it. If it works, you can lift it up bit by bit until your dog is forced to take a jump to get through it. Here, at last, some fur noses might get the splendid idea to crawl underneath the tire or just move around it. That's the point where you need to be resolute and consistent: Give praise and treat only after your dog has dared to jump through the tire.

If your dog's smallish or has short legs, try out which height is the acceptable for him. Bear in mind that his joints are challenged when hitting the ground again after every jump. While the Chi can jump up relatively high because of his light weight, my mixed-breed was a bit clumsier in that respect. With his short legs and long body, it was hard for him to jump up and I soon realized that he felt uneasy with great heights. Well, his short forelegs had to intercept a weight of 10 kilos which isn't that pleasant to do, I guess.

If you're out in training ground, you can see some dogs even jumping through a number of tires. You can train that at a later date and extend your exercise, too, if you wish. But remember that your dog is forced to take a run-up in order to comply with this exercise. Perhaps you position the tires a little detached from each other, so your dog can take another run-up after every tire he jumped through. Anyway, you're relatively free to modify this exercise and you can adjust it to your dog's skills.

❖ *Standing on a stool with all four legs*

Now, it's time for your dog to reach out for airy heights. Ok - I'm exaggerating, but such a stool can be quite high for some dogs.

Your dog is allowed to put his paws on the stool, even when standing, actually, which turns the next step of the exercise to be like child's play. The only thing he needs to do is get his hind legs on the stool.

To keep this exercise on the easy side, pick a stool which your dog can be standing on quite comfortably. If your stool is too small, a big dog, for example, will have to hump his back to be standing on it. That might not be a problem, if this exercise is known to your dog, but in the beginning, he needs abundant space to be able to be standing on it quite normally.

While standing, command your dog to put his fore paws on the stool. After that, you first push the one and then the other hind leg onto the stool. As soon as both legs are on the stool, and he's standing on it, you say the command and reward him for things done well. You might have to show him the procedure several times, but most dogs are quick study.

If he knows his way around, you can vary the height and even size of the stool you use. A dog that perfectly knows the stool-exercise, won't have any problems jumping on a chair and be really high up on it.

But back to the little rascals among the dogs. The stool is a temptation for the dog, no question, particularly when there's something edible on it. Since the dog knows now that he can move up on the stool and that doesn't it mean something negative for him, he might also abuse the situation. Now, it's time to be resolute and consistent again: Say no immediately when you see he's about to jump. Our mixed-breed tried it with the sofa table. As soon as the kiddy stool was placed in front of it, he was up on it in no time. Before we had started this training, he would have never done it in his life.

Some exercises broaden the mental horizon of your dog and, no wonder, that makes him think of certain things he would have never thought of before. I use to talk about that with a chuckle because somehow I even find it cute which thoughts and ideas these lovely fur noses can have in order to reach our delicious human food. As a dog-owner you simply need a large dose of good humour.

❖ *Jumping from a standing position*

Jumping from a standing position can help you refine an exercise, namely that with the disc your dog's supposed to intercept in mid-air. If your dog has reacted by hesitatingly to that exercise, you can train him to jump from a standing position and afterward try again with the flying disc.

I trained that with my dog out of our training action. Whenever he jumped up for joy, I said the "Jump" command and gave him a treat. Unfortunately, I'm at a loss to suggest how it might work otherwise. I also tried it the "normal" way, that is, left him standing first, then showed him a treat while moving it higher and higher. Well, eventually, my dog sat up and begged and being in this position jumped up and down.

Well, that might be another method to teach your dog this behaviour. However, it was my original intention to make him jump from a standing position, and that worked best the way I just told. Perhaps, jumping from a sitting and begging position is an option for working with your dog and for extending your exercises here and there. Have him sit and beg first, then have him run and finally jump up out of the training action.

As above-mentioned, my dog is suffering from back issues for which reason I don't find jumping from a sitting and begging position recommendable for him. But, of course, it's up to you. Decide for yourself, as you please. Just try out both training variants and find out what's easier for your dog in the end.

❖ _Turning around_

This is an exercise which makes definitely sense, if you intend to do dog-dancing. You realize that there are numerous exercises you can use for this purpose, you're right into dog-dancing already. Dog-dancing is something you can teach your dog in passing. What you have to rehearse is your own choreography with him.

But let's go on with this exercise: You can teach your dog out of action or with a treat. When your dog is standing, hold him a treat under his nose. Then you move it sideways along his body, so he must turn his head to follow it with his glance. When holding it over his rear, your fur nose will have to move with his entire body because his neck isn't long enough for turning his head. As soon as he' turning around, you say the "Turn" command and give him his treat.

If your dog likes to spin around before lying down, you can choose that occasion and, say the command and praise him. That's teaching the command out of the daily action, and, moreover, it's so easy-going for you.

Every dog can spin around, that has nothing to do with his body stature and size. Some dogs are very quick; others are rather slow. That's part due to the dog's individual character.

❖ *Waving*

You can teach your dog to wave from a sitting or sitting and beg position. Decide for yourself which variant you prefer. Apart from that, it's a great exercise which you can easily combine with others. If your dog knows how to wave, he will probably even do it when standing, though you will have taught him out of the sitting position.

Command your dog to give his paw and take it in your hand. Then, you lift the paw up and down, just like shaking hands, and give the "Wave" command. Repeat that several times until your dog will do by himself.

Some dogs even tend to hold out their paws to their owner when begging and move them up and down. That's why you could also train him waving out of this particular action. However, it's difficult, if your dog won't try to beg. Well, if that happens, you can be proud of your flawless education.

❖ *Circling for dog-dancing*

Circling is, in a sense, how every dog-dancing starts off. Your dog's moving around you and sits down in front of you. This basic step can be combined with many other elements in the later dancing process.

It's very easy to train your dog to circle. Hold the treat in your hand and show it your dog. Then, move it behind your back, change hands, and move that one back to the front. Your dog will simply follow the treat. When standing in front of you, just say the "Sit" command and complete the exercise. Generally speaking, dogs can be taught circling relatively quickly.

❖ Giving a High Five

Giving your dog a high five! Isn't that a cool idea? Let your dog take the "Sit" position. Now, it's all up to your dog. My dog had been taught to give paw before I started the high five training. So, I didn't hold my hand flat out, but upright, and my dog placed his paw into my hand without much ado. All you need to do is give the "High Five" command.

Shouldn't your dog understand what you want of him right away, hold your hand out to him and take his paw. Put it into your palm and say the command. Later, if your dog knows the command, you can move your hand a bit higher, so your dog must hold out his paw. But to begin with, I'd suggest holding your hand up to your dog's shoulder height which makes this exercise similar to the "give paw" one your dog's familiar with already.

❖ *Kissing hand*

This is another sequence from dog-dancing. Your dog's supposed to lick over your hand in this exercise. Well, it's again up to how your dog reacts. But most dogs really like to lick the outstretched hand of their human friend. If your dog does that by himself, just say the command, so he can combine both elements of the exercise in his mind.

However, if your dog shows no interest whatsoever to lick your hand, you can use a trick that I liked to use to teach my mixed-breed. Spread a tiny bit of liver sausage on your hand where you want your dog to lick it and hold your hand to him. You will see how joyfully he will be kissing your hand. Then, of course, you take advantage of the occasion and say the command. You don't need a treat in this case, the liver sausage on your hand is reward enough for your dog.

But only train this behaviour, if you don't feel unpleasant with it. I know a lot of people who love their dogs, but who don't like being licked in their hands. They consider it unhygienic. I can't understand their behaviour. I just wipe my hands clean with a wet cloth after every training unit. That's it. But, well, that's a question of attitude. In my case, however, I can clearly say that I don't like my dog licking over my face. The same with cats. Several times in the past such kisses were the very cause of bad inflamed pimples in the spots I had been licked. Well, that's something I really don't need to have.

❖ _Moving backward_

This is another exercise from dog-dancing. On your command, your dog must move backwards. That's a behaviour dogs normally show when they're feeling threatened. None of my dogs moves backwards without a reason. If they want to leave, they just turn around and move forward.

You can train moving backwards by approaching your dog and smoothly pushing him backwards. Then, after a few steps, say the "Backward" command. This exercise is well-suited to be combined with others, like for example "Backward" and then "Sit and Beg" or "Backward" and then "Sit". Just be creative how you can keep modifying the exercise. So, it won't get too boring in the long run.

You might wonder about those many dog-dancing steps, but I greatly enjoy them. You're busy with your dog, are able to modify the training routine, and set up your own dog-dancing choreography. I found that this kind of training keeps my dog busy in a very positive way. It never gets boring for him, since every training day is different. He never knows which command comes next which is a main reason for him to stay attentive. However, if you stick to the same routine every day, your dog will get inattentive because he will always know what comes next. This is also a loophole for mistakes. When noticing my dog has become bored and unwilling, I just use another unexpected command and change rules. His reaction shows me, if he's been really mentally busy or if he reacted out of his accustomed routine only.

Level 7

❖ *Moving over the seesaw*

This is a typical exercise from the dog training ground which is meant to train your dog's own sense of balance. If teaching it to a puppy, please be careful. Your puppy could fall off the seesaw and hurt himself. Though, to move up the seesaw, isn't the difficult part of the exercise. It's rather the fact that the seesaw will move down to the other side the moment your dog has passed its middle. Then, he's forced to use his sense of balance or fall off the seesaw.

In order to make your dog familiar with this tool, take him on a short leash and move up and down the seesaw together with him. That means, of course, you walk next to the board while your dog's on it. Let him move up to the middle. Then, take the leash even shorter, which enables you to support your dog. He may then slowly proceed on the seesaw. As soon as it's moving down, your dog will automatically move more slowly and carefully, too. Adjust to his pace and be a good support for him.

If you see your dog is unimpressed with the seesaw, you can optionally lay a trail with a few treats. Place the treats at intervals on the seesaw. In order to get and enjoy them, your dog will have to make his way over the board. That doesn't only distract him, his every step on the seesaw is being rewarded with a treat, too.

Once your dog knows how to behave on the seesaw, he will probably move over it at a faster pace and just having fun with it.

❖ *Moving through a tunnel*

The tunnel is also one of the tools available in the dog training ground, though there are great rustling tunnels for home use as well. Puppies love the tunnel and can't just get enough of it. As far as adult dogs are concerned, it depends on their size. My Chi, for example, has no problems at all moving through the tunnel. But if you have a bigger dog breed, they would have to crawl to reach the other side of the tunnel. It takes them a lot of effort to do it.

If it comes to the tunnel, you can't accompany your dog. He must dare to move through it on his own. Position yourself at the other tunnel opening and call your dog. If you like, you can throw a few treats inside the tunnel, so your dog will feel tempted to enter and move through it.

The sooner you make your dog familiar with the tunnel, the better the chance he will be using it even as a grown-up dog. But please be very patient here, and don't get frustrated too easily, if it takes time to work out as you wish.

❖ _Jumping over smaller obstacles_

We're still in the dog training ground. If your dog knows how to jump through a tire, he won't have problems with obstacles. Start off working with small obstacles he can easily climb over. This is the method to teach him that obstacles don't mean any harm to him.

Later in your training, you can choose to pick higher obstacles. But bear in mind that they need to have a manageable height for your dog.

As an incentive, you can position yourself behind the obstacles with a treat in your hand. So, your dog will be interested in jumping over it and reaching out for your treat.

Even smaller dogs can manage higher obstacles. But if he's not in the right mood for jumping, there is no use. My Chi, for example, doesn't like to jump over obstacles as a rule. So, he would move underneath or around them. Even if we have worked out every obstacle you may find in the dog training ground, he would dodge the jumping obstacles. They might cause him harm or maybe his back hurts when he's jumping, I just don't know the reason. But that's what I'm asking you - never force your dog. If he doesn't want to do something, it isn't a big deal at all. Never work with force. It won't avail to anything. On the contrary, you run the risk of spoiling your dog's pleasure and fun working with you.

❖ *Nudging a football with mouth*

You can't play football with a dog? Yes, you can - and it's nearly perfect! You often watch dog-owners playing football with their dogs. Well, that means in most cases: The human is kicking the ball, and the dog is chasing it. But you can also teach your dog to nudge the ball with his mouth. Needless to say, the ball won't roll far, but it will be rolling anyway.

In order to be able to train that behaviour, your dog needs to have a good relationship with balls in general and really like them. Put a treat under the ball and guide your dog to the ball. Then, point with your finger to the ball, so he will lower his mouth to it. As soon as he's getting the smell of the treat, he will use his mouth to push the ball aside. Don't forget to say the right command.

Well, this exercise might possibly go wrong. My Chi, for example, wouldn't move a thing with his mouth. He uses his paws instead. Yes, he's smelling the treat under the tennis ball, but he uses his fore paw to roll it away. I still train it with him, but it won't work. So, we came to the agreement that he can make this exercise using his paw. Shouting the "Roll Ball" command at him, he would nudge the ball with his paw.

Actually, I don't mean to say that you can't modify this exercise, too. Sometimes, it can make sense to talk things over with your dog. Training should be flexible. But if your dog knows how to do an exercise, you need to stay consistent in what you do. Don't start changing things. These modifications can lead to mistakes in other training exercises and, one day, your dog might not even execute the "Sit" command the way he's supposed to.

❖ *Retrieving garden hose*

Having a helping hand in the garden can never be wrong. Only that your dog must be a water lover. Did you ever try to find out how your dog is reacting when you're turning on the garden hose? Is he jumping joyfully through the jet of water, or is he running off scared? If he loves water, you can teach him to retrieve the garden hose.

He combines a great thing with the garden hose and will love doing it. Take the hose and give it to your dog, so he can take it in his mouth. Say the "Retrieve Hose" command. He knows the retrieve command already, and all he must learn now is what a garden hose is. As soon as it works well, you can extend this exercise. Position yourself a bit far off from the hose and send off your dog. Basically, it's like clearing up toys for your dog.

If your dog is respectful of water, this exercise could fail. Felix doesn't like water and would steer clear of the garden hose. He doesn't even dare to come close. It could go off all of a sudden. In such a case, I don't force the dog to do it. He sees something negative in the garden hose and I can and must accept that.

❖ *Catching a swinging rope*

A swinging rope, perhaps with a ball attached to it, can be a great occupation for dogs. Basically, this exercise is very similar to the one with the flying disc the dog is supposed to intercept in mid-air. He must jump up to do it and, of course, it should be worthwhile for him doing so.

He put up a rod in our garden, to which we fixed a rope. First, there was no ball attached to it, but a chewing rod for dogs. Our dog is loving chewing rods. So, I made the rope swing and my dog tried to fetch the chewing rod. The moment he got it, I said the "Catch Rope" command. Now, there's a tennis ball attached to it and our dog is busy with it all the time we're out in the garden.

Some exercises aren't necessarily laid out for doing something with your dog together. Sometimes, it's about keeping the dog busy with himself without boring him. But since you teach him a command with every exercise, you can actively work with him in this case, too. If you set up an obstacle course in the garden, a task could be to make the ball on the rope swing, so your dog can proceed to the next obstacle in line.

❖ *Taking the lid off the bucket*

This exercise is particularly suitable should you wish to extend it later in your dog training. The dog can take the lid off the bucket and then, get something out of it.

Let your dog execute the "Sit" command in front of the bucket and give him the lid, so he can take it in his mouth. The let him put the lid aside. As soon as the lid is in his mouth, say the "Lid" command. After a few trials you should test, if he can take the lid off the bucket by himself. Needless to say, the lid should be reaching a bit over the edge of the bucket, so you dog can easily fetch it. To provide one more incentive for him, you can put a treat inside the bucket which he can take out as a reward.

Later when your dog knows this exercise, you can include one more training step, namely take the lid away from your dog, put something inside the bucket and then, let him put the lid back onto it. You can be flexible here again and extend the exercises just as you please.

❖ *Dropping and nudging*

Does your dog know how to nudge the ball with his mouth? If yes, extend your exercise with one more command. First, let your dog take the ball, then, command him to drop and nudge it. If your training has been successful so far, your dog should be perfectly aware of all these commands and be able to execute them.

The challenge for the dog here is to do several things in a row. Also, upon releasing it, the ball will roll a few inches on the ground, so your dog will have to go after it.

Later, you can kick the ball and command your dog to retrieve it. Once retrieved, command him to release and nudge it. And you're right in the middle of a game and your dog's got the chance to train his commands. Repeat a few things and then proceed with another exercise.

❖ *Digging hole*

This is no-go in the garden, but perhaps your dog's got his own green area for romping about. To dig a hole is something many dogs quite naturally do, such as my Chi, who would hide his treasures in it. Also, his favourite toy, which I searched for many days.

If your dog likes to dig, you can teach him the command out of your daily training action. When he's digging somewhere, just say "Dig" and praise him. Unless dig a small hole, place a treat inside and cover it with earth. Then you send off your dog to get his treat. He will start digging to uncover it, while you say the command right at the beginning of his action. Bear in mind, the treat should be rather big in size. Otherwise, he might dig it deeper into the ground.

However, I have to address a few words of warning to you here: This exercise can go wrong. If your dog is a real digger and you allow him to do it, he might start digging in places in your garden that are off limits for him. Your dog won't make a difference. He doesn't care, if it's his place in the garden or your flowerbed. In such a case, say the "Stop" command and take him to the place he's allowed to dig in. Then, just command "Dig".

Well, sometimes things can be quite difficult with these exercises, since, basically, you let him do things he's not allowed to do at all. He makes no difference and doesn't understand why he can dig here and can't dig there. But always take it easy. In the end, it so cute to see this fur nose digging like crazy, the earth flying away to all sides and your dog coming out of it with a black face.

❖ *Crawling on the ground*

Dogs in police shows do it, and your dog can do it, too: Crawling on the ground.

Should your dog be a tunnel crawler, he will know how to do that already. However, he doesn't know the proper command that goes with it. You can best train that as follows: Command your dog "Down" and hold a treat in your hand which is touching the ground. Now, your dog must get down with his head. The moment he's about to get it, you pull your hand away. He will have to stretch his neck and, all of a sudden, be prompted to crawl after the treat. Then it's time to say your command.

Optionally, you can train that by letting him crawl under a given obstacle. But command him "Down" first to prevent him from jumping over the obstacle. The good thing about obstacles and tunnels is that your dog is always bound to crawl to reach his treat.

This exercise is ideal for changing your training ground routine every once in a while, and make things more thrilling, so your dog won't be bored in the long run.

Level 8

❖ *Jumping over higher obstacles*

If your dog knows how to jump, raise the level of your training and use obstacles with a greater height. For your dog it will mean much more effort, and that's exactly what he needs for a proper workout.

But always consider the size of your dog. As mentioned several times before, you can demand more of a German Shepherd than of a pug. Also, it depends on your dog's height, if he can jump out of the running or off some higher obstacle.

❖ *Pushing a skateboard*

The sole purpose of this exercise is to keep your dog busy. Sometimes it's just about doing something together with your dog and keeping him busy without putting much training sense into it. If your dog is a particularly quick study and dares to tread on a moving skateboard, you can also use this exercise to train his sense of balance.

Place one or two of his paws on the skateboard, so he's got the chance to get used to it. This exercise is very similar to training your dog to put his paw on a stool. If it works well with him, give your dog a light push from behind, and he will have to make a few steps with his hindlegs. Then say the "Push" command. He will know fairly quickly what you demand of him and start pushing himself.

If you see your dog's afraid of the situation, don't do the exercise or don't force him to do it.

❖ *Up and down the seesaw*

Does your dog know his way around the seesaw in the dog training ground by now? If yes, you can now make things a bit more difficult for him. Don't let him walk over it and get off again but let him walk up and down the seesaw.

Use the target stick for that purpose. When your dog is on the seesaw, tap the spot he's supposed to go to and stop. After that, you tap another spot. Thus, you can make your dog run up and down the board.

Well, we've come quite a long way now and have begun with easy exercises. Meanwhile you will certainly have gained a good expertise how to train this exercise with your dog successfully. There are several things to be found in the dog training ground whose function is rather hard to explain. Best you try out yourself how you can best make your dog familiar with them.

❖ *Extending the football match*

If you wish to play football with your dog in an active manner, be careful not to bump into each other. It happens so quick that your dog fetches your leg instead of the ball, and you don't kick the ball, but your dog. So, keep a certain distance to each other when playing football.

You can kick the ball back and forth between the two of you. Another option is to kick the ball and send off your dog to get it. Your dog will have the chance to roll the ball to you by nudging it with his mouth. Or he can retrieve it to you in his mouth.

Think creatively about further exercises you could include into your training routine, so the football match will simultaneously be a kind of command-training for your dog.

❖ _Holding the garden hose while the dog pool is being filled up with water_

Your dog can hardly wait to see his dog pool filled up with water, and he's so keen on jumping right into it? If yes, he can be of some assistance in this process.

He knows your garden hose already, and he knows how to retrieve it to you. Now, let your dog get the garden hose and execute the "Sit and Stay" command with the hose in his mouth in front of the pool. Adjust the hose in his mouth in such a manner as to prevent it from splashing into his mouth. Then, turn on the water.

Then, it's time to give your dog a good amount of praise and release him into the refreshing cool water. But surely, there are dogs that just can't wait to get into the pool. In such a case let your dog get into it first. Then, you can give him the garden hose.

Well, it's not important if or if not the dog fills up the pool with the garden hose. If he holds the hose in his mouth for a short while, that's fine. Bear in mind that you can't extend this exercise indefinitely, since your dog might find it too stupid sooner or later.

❖ _Putting the lid on the bucket_

It's no longer a big deal for your dog to take the lid off the bucket? If yes, you can now show him to put the lid back onto it. Give him the lid or let him take it off the ground. Hold the bucket under the lid and command the dog to release it. Upon releasing, you say the "Lid on" command. After a few trials, it should be working well. On your command, your dog will put the lid back onto the bucket, though it's standing on the ground.

You might need some patience with this exercise because the incentive to take off the lid and to reach the treat was much stronger - he was so curious to see what's inside the bucket. When choosing the lid bear in mind that your dog's supposed to take it off the ground without problems. In case of doubt, attach a handle to the lid. If the lid's made of plastic, you can easily fix it by means of bolt and nut. Sometimes you need some help which you may find attached to many dog toys from the pet supplies shop.

❖ _Moving over a narrow rack in the dog training ground_

When moving on the rack, your dog must be balancing his weight. You can train that in the woods, for example, by using an overturned tree trunk. This exercise is aimed at training your dog's sense of balance and concentration. At the same time, it's a training of personal trust because in the beginning you will have to act as a kind of back up for your dog in order to prevent him from falling off the trunk.

Should your dog be afraid of the rack or the trunk, hold him by his breast harness and take him on a very short leash. That's how you can be his back-up in case of a misstep. Being next to him, let your dog move slowly up and down the rack. Your dog will determine the pace. Having reached the other side of the rack, give him a big praise or a treat.

As soon as your dog knows his way around the rack, he can walk up and down on it by himself. In the beginning you may walk next to him. Later, however, you should be waiting for your dog at the other side of the rack.

The training rack can be found in the dog training ground and often features in dog sport events. Needless to say, these events are about timing as well. But if your dog has mastered the rack exercise, he will be able to move up and down the board fairly fast. That's why you should in any case use your walks through the woods for including the trunk exercise into your routine.

Later you may extend this exercise and let your dog jump in a zigzag manner over the rack which, however, will be a bit more difficult for him to accomplish. So go for it only if your dog knows exactly how to move over the rack.

❖ *Moving up a ladder*

It's much easier to do the ladder exercise with a big dog than with a small breed. Having a small dog, you have to find the right ladder whose steps are close enough for the size of the dog.

For the dog to become familiar with the ladder, you should place it on the ground and let your dog run over it several times. And put a treat on every step, if your like. The treat will be incentive enough to make him more or less automatically move up and down the ladder. If it works with your dog, position the ladder upright, though it shouldn't be too steep for your dog. Put a treat on the upmost step, so your dog must stretch his body to reach it. He will probably have to put his fore paws on the step he can reach most easily with his body. After that, he will try to put his hindlegs on a lower step.

Pick a treat that he's really in love with which will add up the incentive. Watch the position of the ladder. In no case should it be too steep, that means, your dog shouldn't be forced to climb it up vertically. If it's a bit steeper than the seesaw, that's fine. But bear in mind when doing this exercise: Safety first! If your dog slips off the step, he could hurt himself seriously when hitting the hard ground.

❖ _"Dead Dog" command_

This is another great out-of-action exercise. If your dog relaxes, he's lying down on the side, head on the ground and stretching out both legs. Doing so, say the "Dead Dog" command and give him a treat. This exercise is a great one for your dog because, basically, relaxing is a positive thing for him. And if you reward him for doing it, he will like this exercise even better.

Of course, you can train this behaviour separately. Tickle your dog while he's lying. When he's feeling comfortable and turning on his side, say the command. That's a method to combine both cuddling and training.

My Chi, for example, doesn't do the roll exercise anymore. His back will cause him too much pain, but he really likes to execute the "Dead Dog" command. In most cases, I'm sure he's got the idea in his mind to stay in exactly that that position for ever. And only grudgingly, he would be prepared to get up again and be ready for more exercises. That's why I usually do the "Dead Dog" exercise towards the end of our training units. If he's still lying on the ground, he will get his tickles and can relax as he pleases. That's how you can take advantage of the end of your daily training routine. So, the end of the day, your dog will be really satisfied and have the feeling that your training was worth it.

❖ *Opening a door*

Big dogs are true experts in opening doors. Smaller breed have their problems. We live in a 200-year-old house with big, heavy wooden doors. For our dog they are a big obstacle, and he really won't make it to push them open. So, Felix doesn't make it. Our mixed-breed on the other hand did have the necessary weight to push against the doors, yet couldn't reach the door handle.

We fastened a rope to the door handle. So, he had to pull at it in order to open the door. After that, he could open it with his mouth, or he pulled at the rope until the door was ajar. With small dogs, this trick works only if the door opens inward. So, even if the dog pulled at the rope, he wouldn't be able to open a door opening outward. Automatically, he would close the door when pulling on the rope. Well, you could teach your dog how to close the door instead.

A big dog, on the other hand, is able to push the door handle down with his paw while in the begging position. That means for such a dog, doors opening outward are a better choice to work with. He can open it almost automatically using his body weight. Bear that in mind before you start your training, so your efforts will be successful in the end.

Also bear in mind that a big dog that has mastered this exercise could theoretically open the door to your house. It's recommendable to take whatever precautions necessary, otherwise you might be returning home one day and find the door to your house wide open.

Does your dog know the "Catch Rope" exercise? If yes, it won't be a problem to teach him how to push down the door handle. As soon as he's opened the door, you say the "Open Door" command and reward him for complying.

If you've got a big dog, let him sit and beg in front of the door handle first. Then, he's to put his paw on the handle, just like doing the stool exercise. You can be of assistance to your dog by placing your hand on his paw that's resting on the handle already. Then, help him pushing it down smoothly. The moment the handle is down, say the command and let go.

Some dogs are a quick study and know very fast how the door's opening. Our mixed-breed was clever and knew exactly, if he had to push with his paw or pull with his mouth to open the door. My Chi, however, stops in front of the door most of the times and starts barking, even when it's ajar. He attempts to push the door, but as we can judge from his efforts, he just won't make it. Yet he's on the lucky side, if the cats want to enter the room, too. Thanks to their 6 kilos of living weight, it's really no problem for them to open the doors. So, Felix just runs after them.

Level 9

❖ *Reading and following up tracks*

Basically, this exercise can be taught to every dog. Hunting and working dogs, however, will be having great fun and need to use their brains. Reading tracks means true work for nose and head. It's really heavy work for your dog. After such an exercise, your dog will be in need of a break, and you shouldn't send him off to follow up tracks that are too long.

You can work together with a helping hand, or you go check the walking route prior to your training routine and use the opportunity to lay some trails. Of course, you can start small and lay a trail inside your own house.

For the purpose of home trails, you can take various cardboard boxes with a lid. Hide, for example, a piece of cloth with a certain distinct smell inside such a box and hold another piece of cloth with the same smell under your dog's nose. Has he absorbed the smell, you guide him to the boxes and say the "Search" command which he should know by now. Your dog will start sniffing at the boxes to find the right box with the cloth inside. Has he got it, he will signal it to you, that is, might bark or tug with his paw at the box.

In order to extend and modify this exercise at a later date, you may ask somebody to lay a trail for you in the woods. Since this person will be the one to check the route, his smell will be there, too. Then, the same person will have to deposit a piece of cloth that he had had on him and return the same way he'd come. In the meantime, you're waiting together with your dog at the starting-point of the exercise. As soon as the said person has come back to you, your dog will be released to sniff at the person and absorb his smell. Then you give the "Search" command, and your dog will try to find the right track and be hopefully successful finding the piece of cloth in the end.

Basically, reading tracks is no big deal for dogs because they have a very fine nose. But following them up they might be distracted by many other smells and impressions from their environment. My Chihuahua, for example, isn't into reading tracks very much. He can find his treats that I hide somewhere, no problem, but he has never been willing to go after a trail in the woods. My mixed-breed, on the other hand, who was a Dachshund-Spitz, had the trail reading instincts in his veins. Except for a few occasions, he would always find what my husband had tried hard to hide for him somewhere.

❖ *Moving between the legs in a certain sequence and with help of a target stick. Preparatory to the commands "Go backwards", "Spin" and "Turn around".*

Now we're coming back to dog-dancing. You have taught your dog several steps already. Does your dog know how to run through pylons, this exercise will be like child's play for him.

Stand with legs apart and let your dog be standing in front of you. Now, starting off from the front he's supposed to move between your legs: First, around your left leg, then passing you at the front, around the right leg, and from behind back between your legs to finish the exercise standing in front of your again. Well, of course, you can change the sequence of this exercise, as you wish. For example, it's easy to extend this exercise by including other dog-dancing steps.

How to start? You have to get your dog moving because he must know the direction. Then, take a treat in your hand and hold it behind your left leg, so your dog can clearly see it. As soon as your dog has run between your legs, your hand is moving the treat to the front and to your right leg. Then, as soon as he's standing next to your right leg, you must hold the treat between your legs so the dog feels tempted to move right between them and, eventually, come back to the front. If he knows the hand signs, it will work out quite well even without using a treat at a later time. In that case it will be sufficient for you to use your finger as a pointer.

❖ *Working off the tools in the dog training ground one by one*

I'm sure your training in the dog training ground is progressing well. Now you may try to work off the entire training ground with your dog. If you like, you can stop the time it takes because dog sport events are also about timing and swiftness.

In the beginning you will have to run along with your dog and accompany him to the next obstacle, so he learns the various training routes. Yes, you might get out of breath very soon, especially if your dog is a swift one and leaving the obstacles behind him like nothing. But it will be great fun being with him, and in the end, you will realize that everything was done right. A matter of pride, no doubt!

❖ _Balancing out on the seesaw_

I suggested this option to you above, should you wish to extend the seesaw challenge. Let your dog move up to the middle of the seesaw. Watch out, he's not supposed to move too far so the seesaw won't tilt.

That's not so easy a task and a matter of minute work for your dog. One step too many and the seesaw is out of balance. Best you guide your dog by his harness because it's handy for you to correct his movements. As soon as the seesaw is balanced out, let him be standing there for a short while. This exercise is good for training his sense of balance.

❖ *Climbing a ladder and using a slide*

If there is such an obstacle available in your dog training ground, don't miss it out. How to get on a ladder, he will have learned already in another exercise. Now, he's supposed to climb it, remain standing on the landing and after your "Down" command rush down the slide. The slide is a particular challenge for a dog, which he might be even afraid of. If he's unwilling to do it, don't force him to use this obstacle, but try another method to get him off again.

It may work with an especially fine treat to make your dog lie down and take the slide down.

❖ *Extending the "Dead Dog" command*

Your dog knows this exercise already and is probably quite well-behaved. But as it gets boring fairly quickly, you can combine it with several other exercises. The best option would be to combine it with exercises to be made in the lying position.

Command your dog "Down", then "Dead Dog" and after that, say the "Roll" command. This is another exercise you can adapt as you please. Of course, you have to let your dog finish one exercise before you start the next one. Otherwise, he might get confused about what you want him to do.

❖ _Using the light switch on command_

Should you have a big dog, this is something he will certainly master. No question. Did you teach him to push down the door handle? If yes, show him to put his paw a little more up on the handle in order to reach the light switch and say the "Light" command. This exercise is no problem at all, if you have toggle switches in your house.

Careful! If there is a plug positioned right underneath the light switch, refrain from doing this exercise with your dog - or you may fix a child lock to the plug before you start. Otherwise, your dog may suffer from an electric shock when reaching into the plug with his paw.

❖ _Bringing things, for example a ringing phone_

Your dog can facilitate your daily life, such as assistance dogs are meant to. You can teach him to bring you certain things. To be successful with this exercise, you will have to train it with the same object until he exactly knows what to do.

If you want him to bring you the ringing phone, let it ring first, then give it to him and say the "Bring" command or whatever command you have taught your dog for this kind of exercise.

After a few training units you dog will bring the ringing phone on your command. Bear in mind, however, that his sharp teeth may cause damage to certain objects. If you've got a very expensive and fragile phone, you better avoid this exercise. A touchscreen phone, for example, could be seriously damaged.

❖ *Sorting things, balls to balls, sticks to sticks.*

Sorting games are a big challenge for your dog's mind. It might not work straight away, but if you start off small, he will make it. No doubt.

It's important for your dog to know the names of the things in question. For example, scatter several balls on the ground across the room. He's supposed to get all the balls and put them on a pile. Use the commands you've taught your dog. If it works, you can put one more object on the ground. Thus, you can extend this exercise object by object.

The more objects there are on the ground, the harder for your dog to accomplish his task. He will surely make mistakes and take the wrong thing. Should it happen, you're there to correct him.

❖ *Picking up things that fell on the ground.*

Since you can't name all things that are in your house to your dog, this exercise is a rather general one. Your dog must learn to react on the "Pick up" command.

Point to the object in question on the ground and let him take it into his mouth. In case of doubt, give him the said object, if he doesn't want to take it up himself. As soon as it's in his mouth, you say the command. Then, you give him the "Retrieve" command.

Since your dog doesn't know what's supposed to remain on the ground and what he's supposed to pick up, you have to point actively with your finger or use the target stick.

Level 10

❖ *Running between the legs in a certain manner*

It's time for the next dog dancing round! As explained to you above, you can let your dog run between your legs in whatever manner you wish. The sequence is up to you. Now, it's time to conceive of the next dog-dancing choreography.

Active dog-dancing requires the human dancing partners to move along with their dogs, which means, it's you who determines the very sequence the dog is supposed to run between your legs, and, while doing so, you're moving forward step by step. Your dog is entitled to keep his fixed direction. That's why it's important to teach him to keep the same direction during dog-dancing. He must know it before you start the training. Then try to move along with the dancing steps. Caution! Both of you have a really good chance to trip here! Best you make slow steps and try to keep your legs sufficiently apart, so your dog can run between them without difficulty.

Ideally, you move one step forward whenever your dog has re-emerged from between your legs and is standing next to you or behind you.

❖ *Following up longer trails*

Reading tracks should be further developed step by step. If you start off your training laying a trail with a length of several hundred meters, it might just be too much for your dog. Proceed slowly. Try shorter trails first, as described in the context of the basic exercise. After that, you may, for example, lay a trail into another room inside your house.

Later, if you go out with your dog, you lay trails at greater intervals. It's important that there will be a reward for your dog at the point of destination. But then you should call it a day and terminate your training. Your dog will need a break and must have the chance to relax.

❖ *On the skateboard*

Can your dog put his paw on the skateboard and push it? If yes, allow him to move his entire body on it. Leave it to your dog's decision, if the board is in motion or standing still. Some dogs are afraid of a moving board and get off again immediately.

Let your dog go on the skateboard like he went on the stool. Then, you push the board slowly forward and try how your dog's behaving. If he likes it, it's fine. If he wants to get off again immediately, accept it.

Basically, this exercise is about fun, you're not training your dog to join some circus event. It's simply about doing something together and, of course, having fun all the time.

❖ *Carrying the shopping basket*

There are dogs that have great fun carrying a stick or ball in their mouth all the way along their daily walking route, while others drop things again quite quickly and don't even dream of carrying them somewhere. But it's possible to teach that behaviour to your dog.

Give him a basket and let him take it with his mouth. Then, you walk a bit or as long as he's willing to carry the basket. While you're walking, repeat the "Carry" command. As soon as he's putting the basket somewhere, you make a short break or say commands like "Sit" or "Look" as a kind of interim-exercise. Then, you give the basket back to him and start again at the beginning.

In the beginning, he might just carry the basket all the way down, or perhaps you must make a break in-between. It completely depends on your dog. Later in the exercise, you can replace the basket by a stick or a ball or, optionally, put a toy inside the basket.

❖ *Getting the newspaper from outside the front door and bringing it*

Now, it's time for your dog to be of some assistance to you. For this exercise to accomplish properly, he must know what a newspaper is and, ideally, put it in front of your main door.

Show your dog the newspaper and give it to him. Then say the "Newspaper" command. As soon as he's got it in his mouth, you command him to bring it to you.

For a later exercise you can put the newspaper somewhere on the ground and command your dog to get and bring it. If it works, you can try this exercise using the morning newspaper in front of your main door. Open the main door to your dog or let him open it by himself. Then, send him off to get your newspaper.

The only thing you have to do is tell the postman not to put it in the mailbox or the newspaper roll. Otherwise, your dog can't get it for you.

❖ *Finishing the dog training ground as quickly as possible*

I do like the dog training ground. I don't join dog competitions, but it's simply a great place to train your dog and include new elements into your schedule.

Your dog should be familiar with all tools he can master and know how to handle them. Then, it's time to work with the time factor for a change. Determine a route your dog's supposed to take and show it to him several times. This route should be working perfectly. Release your dog and don't miss to cheer him on. The purpose of this exercise is to improve the timing of your training. Thus, your exercises are like a sporting event for your dog he can use to let off steam.

❖ *The fixed dog-dancing procedure*

You might have thought a bit more about the subject of "dog-dancing" and taught your dog some exercises which are not described in this book.

Combine your own choreography now and train it with your dog several times. In the end, you won't have to tell him a lot, he will know exactly what to do. Off you go! Perform your latest choreo!

You're invited to enter into this subject a little more comprehensively, if you like. There are many different dog-dancing sequences possible, and your dog will never be bored.

Did you know that there are real dog-dancing events where the dog-teams compete against each other? This might be a great idea for the two of you to prove your skills to others. As said before, there are many recommendable guides available which deal with all these subjects and provide many valuable tips and incentives for the work with your dog.

❖ *Dog bowling, dog must push football at bottles*

Dog bowling may not be something special for your dog, but it makes your training routine much more thrilling. To Fill up a few empty bottles with water to make them stand fast and position them like bowling pins.

Your dog has learned to nudge the ball with his nose on command. So, you put the ball in front of the bottles. The distance between the bottles should depend on how hard your dog is pushing the ball. You better try out how far the ball's rolling when your dog's pushing it.

Then, let your dog stand in front of the ball and say the "Push" command. If you like, you can command your dog to retrieve the fallen pins to you. Then, put the ball back in its place and start the game again.

In order to provide another incentive for his senses, you can now play a round. Your dog must comply with the "Sit and Stay" command and should be watching closely what you're doing. The fact that you're playing right now is a matter of a big distraction for him and he would certainly very much like to run after the ball. But that's exactly the purpose of this exercise: He's supposed to remain in the "Sit" position until you give the release command. After you played a round, it's your dog's turn and he's being rewarded right away because he's getting the ball back. Bear in mind that those distraction exercises are important to teach your dog to behave controlled.

❖ *Toys for training your dog's intelligence: Putting forms into fitting openings*

Sometimes you certainly want your dog to be occupied with himself in a sensible way because you might have no time for him or simply be working. Toys for training intelligence are a great solution. Check out what's available in the pet supplies shops. You will find a good choice of toys.

You may pick a toy like this: A game board with ready-made forms which are removable and have got a handle, so your dog can easily fetch it with his mouth. Now, he's supposed to put the right form into the fitting openings. You will have to train that with your dog, and I'm warning you, some dog may never make it. That's purely a mind toy for your dog that requires your dog to recognize things clearly and have a good sense of coordination.

Many special working breeds master these intelligence toys like child's play, and they are really fast to learn how things function. But these dog breeds prefer to work with their head. I don't mean to say that other dog breeds are stupid compared to them, they just have their strengths elsewhere which brings us back to the subject, and that is, to further and challenge your dog according to his racial skills.

Of course, this game is just a suggestion. You may choose another one. As said, have a look around in shops. There are really a lot of different games available that are categorized according to levels of difficulty. That gives you the chance to raise the level as you wish. Some of these games are modular by nature. For example, you buy a Level One game and work up with your dog to Level Three or more. Look out for such a game in the shop, though it doesn't really matter in a sense. Every game is interesting in itself and it makes no difference in the end, if you've got a number of games at your disposal or only separate game boards. Yet it's important for you to know in the beginning what the game is basically about, so you can train your dog accordingly.

❖ *Intelligence toy: Carrying treat through a maze*

As a rule, you can say, most dogs really like these toys. There's something fine in there for them, and they don't have to wait too long for their reward. These toys are available in different models as well. I for myself, for example, find the game board-maze fairly interesting. You place the treat in the opening, and your dog's supposed to use his mouth or paws to push it all the way through the passages until he reaches the other side of the maze. When done correctly, the treat will fall off from the game board in the end.

Optionally, there are such treat-games where the treat is hidden behind doors or under boxes and your dog's supposed search for them and open the respective compartments. As a rule, there are handles and bands attached to these compartments, so your dog can open them with his mouth. These treat-games can also be laid out in different categories as far as the level of difficulty is concerned, ranging from easy to difficult.

My Chi, for example, has got such a treat-game where there are many lids on the game boards. Treats can be hidden under these lids. If I hide a treat under two of these lids, he will find them on the spot and remove the lid with his paw. I think most dogs know how to operate that. And if they are as greedy as my Chi, for example, these games would be just child's play for them.

We also have a treat-ball which will release its fine contents only if it's properly turned around by the dog. Felix loves to play that, too. By now, he knows how to spin and turn the ball to get the treat out. He can be fully occupied with this ball when, for example, we're not at home for some time. The cats love it, too.

You have to know in advance that you may buy this or that intelligence toy which your dog won't like to play with, or which poses no secret for him right away. Of course, that's no good. The latter case, however, means that your dog is going to be bored by it very quickly. The better you know your dog, the better you can reckon which toy might be the best one for him. You may look these toys up on the Net. There are many instruction manuals online that tell you how to build such a toy yourself. Not only is it pure fun, but you can also save a lot of money because very often you can use objects, tools or appliances you've got at home.

Now, I hope I could give you many great incentives for the many training hours you might still be ahead for the two of you. Keep patient and remain consistent. But always bear in mind that everything has to work without the application of force or violence. If you can't teach your dog an exercise and if it won't work even after many more trials, just accept it. There are exercises that just don't fit to the character of your dog. That's nothing to worry about. You don't like every game you can play with other people, either, while others you're really fond of playing. Your dog's about the same. He's not supposed to like everything because, to be honest, the training is supposed to be good fun for the two of you in the end. If he's really into a task, you will always reach the goal of your training. If he's rather unwilling and appears to be listless, things will turn out to be frustrating for both of you. In such a case, just change the exercise or call it a day. You dog is allowed to have a bad day, too, and shouldn't be supposed to be happy all the time.

Whenever my Chi withdraws into his basket after our daily walk and his breakfast, I know he's having a bad day. As a matter of fact, he would be very moody and bark at every dog he's meeting outside. He would be absolutely unwilling to do his exercises and I would have to correct him very often or he will simply stay completely passive. On a day like that he's only interested in cuddles and playing. I know that and I do accept it, and in such cases, I would never force him to do something. In the beginning I thought he wouldn't be serious and despite his reactions I made plans for our daily routine. Today, I know that things are not always working as scheduled and that I simply have to accept that my dog needs to have his break and quietude every once in a while.

Not wishing to hold you up any longer, I'm closing here, since I presume you want to try out new exercises with your dog. So have much fun and go ahead!

The Clicker Training

The clicker is a great assistance tool and makes your dog execute your commands even more precisely. In the dog sport field, the clicker has passed all tests, but many dog-owners use it for their private purposes as well. For the clicker training to work, your dog must learn to understand the clicker and its purpose. And you have to know how to handle this small tool because it's important for you to clicker right on spot, which is easier said than done.

That's why you should rehearse with your clicker. Drop a tennis ball or let somebody else drop it for you. The moment the ball's touching the ground, you press the clicker. That's the way it will be later in the context of your dog training units. You've got about two seconds. If you praise your dog or clicker too late, your dog won't be able to combine the sound with what he's done and know why he's being rewarded. So, the clicker is an excellent training method, since you're faster pressing it than saying "Great", which means, you can react to your dog's training success much faster and better.

As soon as you know how to operate the clicker, show it to your dog. Press it while giving him a treat. That's called "Classic Conditioning". You teach your dog that the clicking sound is followed by something positive. That's why the clicker training makes so much sense in dog training. Your dog will learn very quickly that the clicker sound will be heard only if something was done right. In the course of the training, you can sooner or later leave out the treat as a reward for your dog.

The Conditioning

Everything starts off with the conditioning of your dog. With a treat bag and your clicker, you take your dog to a place where there is at least distraction for him as possible. Here the conditioning process can take place. But it's not yet the right time to train commands. Starting off, you're walking across a field, clicker and give him a treat which you repeat about 20 times: Clicker-Treat-Clicker-Treat ...

Give the treat immediately after the clicker sound, but avoid talking to your dog, exchanging glances and showing him the clicker. The conditioning needs to happen casually.

If or if not, your conditioning efforts have been successful, you may have to test later. Wait until your dog's fully occupied with something else, then you press the clicker. Should he react to the sound and is he looking at you attentively, you have taught him the clicker successfully. But bear in mind never to use the clicker in order to draw your dog's attention to you. The clicker is a confirmation marker and will always be used in connection with a treat or something like a thorough praise. Remember that your dog's not supposed to see a kind of reward in the clicker.

You can start off with clicker training when your dog's still a puppy. Regardless of if puppy or adult dog, keep calm, even if your dog shouldn't understand right away what you're demanding of him.

I used the clicker for my first dog, however, when he was a bit older. It took some time until he got it, but after that, it went just great. My second dog, on the other hand, got to know the clicker as a puppy. But I had to find out that some exercises were still too difficult for him, or I was too slow on the clicker. Sometimes he was even too quick for my me and my clicker, so I put it back into the cupboard. I only got back to the clicker when I started teaching him the exercises.

It worked well with all my dogs. As far as my first dog is concerned, however, the training was later done by means of hand signs because he had gone hard of hearing in his later days and couldn't hear the clicker sound any more. Basically, he had to learn everything new, so I had to teach him hand signs for the most important commands which, luckily enough, he got fairly quickly. But I could let him off leash on big meadows because it would have been impossible to call him back otherwise.

Troubleshooting Clicker Training

Using the clicker, you can make a lot of mistakes, often without being aware of them, which complicate your dog's learning process. Needless to say, the exercises shouldn't be too difficult. Don't overstrain your dog and use the clicker only when exercising things your dog actually knows how to accomplish. But there's another big problem that I mentioned before, and that's if you press the clicker too early or too late. Make sure your dog has successfully undergone the basic conditioning process and train it with him as long as necessary. Avoid speaking while working with the clicker. So don't clicker and praise at the same time, but clicker only. This sound is the reward for your dog.

Two Variants of Clicker Training

You can use the clicker in two different ways: First, you can focus on certain exercises, or you can make use of natural behavioural pattern. And you can combine both variants, if you wish.

If you want to make use of your dog's natural behaviour, it's imperative for you to watch your dog closely. As soon as he's holding out his forelegs, you press the clicker and say the "Bow" command. Then you give him a treat. Do it several times when he's holding out his extremities, and he will have learned a command - without the need for a complex training unit.

I for myself enjoy this kind of clicker training very much because the end of the day the dog is able to perform feats which you might have never able to teach him otherwise.

However, if you wish to form his behaviour more freely, you have to teach certain commands to your dog, as described at length in the previous Training Schedule. As soon as he's in the "Sit" position, you press the clicker and give him his treat.

As said above, you can combine both clicker training variants very effectively and teach your dog some "treats", like for example in the context of dog-dancing. This dog sport is an ideal opportunity to use the clicker. The same applies to the dog training ground with its tubes, ramps and jumping walls.

As far as clicker training is concerned, I recommend you get yourself informed more thoroughly, so you may see which options you have at your disposal.

Problems with Clicker Training

Sometimes things just don't want to work as scheduled. There can be numerous reasons. The most common reasons, however, are explained in the following:

> ➤ *The dog doesn't concentrate*

This is a problem you would often encounter with young dogs. They just run around, are inattentive, and appear unwilling to work with the clicker. One reason could be the choice of the treat. If the treat is too tasty, your dog will be perfectly happy with it, and, naturally, he won't see any point in trying to get more of it. Better pick a treat which is less attractive to your dog.

Another reason could be overstraining the dog. Perhaps, you've been out practising for quite a long time, and he simply needs a break, or the exercise is still too difficult for him. Take a break, let your dog run around as he pleases and postpone the harder exercises on a later date. In case of exercises that are difficult for your dog, you should think about realistic options to make them easier, so you're able to teach him slowly step by step. But never forget that the clicker training is something completely new for your dog, too. The clicking sound alone might overstrain him after a certain time of practice.

> ## *The dog doesn't enjoy the training*

It's a fact that not every dog enjoys the clicker training, some dogs just can't cope with it. There are dogs that, as a rule, don't like to train and, consequently, are unwilling to respond to your efforts. A working dog, for example, doesn't see any sense in dog training exercises at all. He would rather like to be searching for something or guarding it. Therefore, think about your exercises and find out, if they're really making sense for the dog breed you've got. The Beagle, for example, is a tracker dog. He's absolutely happy with reading tracks, whereas dog-dancing is not the right choice for many Beagles, to be honest. They just don't feel at ease with it.

Also bear in mind that your own mood can be easily transferred on the dog. If you're stressed or if you don't feel like training your dog, drop it. Your mood is being transferred on the dog which means that he won't feel like doing exercises and will be rather unwilling like yourself.

> ## *My dog is doing the previous trick*

That may happen and shows you how clever your four-legged friend is. He successfully accomplished the previous exercise and got his treat - so why not repeating the same trick to get more treats.

In such a case, you need to stay consistent and ignore the trials of your dog. If he really doesn't want to make the exercise you want him to execute, why not change the place and start again somewhere else. For a dog, a change of location means something like a new start.

> ## *We got stuck in the middle of a trick*

That's something, however, you have to do some serious troubleshooting for. Your dog might still not understand the steps of the exercise or know them by heart. Perhaps you're teaching the wrong way, so he can't really understand. Or he might simply be overworked. Best you go back to the last training point you're sure your dog has got. Then you take it from there. But proceed with smaller working steps and think about the options you have to change your teaching method.

Sometimes it's like in the human world - the solution is so close at hand, and we don't have a clue and can't continue.

I found out that some dogs can be taught much faster, if they can use their paws, while others prefer to work with their mouth. Try to find out which group your dog's belonging to. Mouth training means you have to use your finger as a pointer to show your dog where to go and what to do, and he would be entitled to tap it with his mouth. Just run a test which method is easier for your four-legged friend.

> ## *My dog is afraid of the clicker*

It's quite common thing that dogs are afraid of the sound or can get irritated by it. I suggest testing the clicker straight in the pet supplies shop. Some of them are very loud, while others have got a rather low sound. Another option is to put the clicker in your coat pocket, so the sound will be muffled. That's a good idea, by the way, because your dog's not supposed to see the clicker anyway. As soon as you finished the conditioning process, your dog knows the sound and has become used to it. Then, there would be no problem anymore using the clicker outside your coat pocket. Your dog will know that the sound means something positive for him. He will be happy hearing it since it's promising him another treat in the end.

> ### *My dog only reacts to hand signs, but not to spoken commands*

That happens fairly often, the reason being that it's much easier to teach dogs things visually than verbally. Always bear in mind that all dogs communicate by means of their body language when being together in their pack. That's why he prefers to react to gestures, hand signs or your facial expressions and not so much to what you're saying. That's the reason why I taught a hand sign for every command to all of my dogs. When my first dog became hard of hearing, I was so happy he could at least still understand my hand signs.

All of which doesn't mean you should be gesticulating like crazy all the time. Yes, your dog can understand you verbally, even if he doesn't like it that much. Rehearse that trick with him several times and without taking a break. Prior to every trick you give the "Sit" command. Rehearse, rehearse, and rehearse again, and, above all, avoid using hand signs. As soon as your dog knows how to execute your command, give him an especially fine treat. That works like a reconfirmation for him, and he will soon know how to do the exercise without hand signs. Just be a bit patient with him.

Of course, eventually, you have to decide for yourself, if you want to educate your dog with commands or hand signs or either of these methods. Generally speaking, your hand signs aren't a wrong choice at all, but you have to consider that your dog must learn to comply with your verbal call back command. The same, for example, applies to the "Drop" command. Some hand signs are simply being ignored in the heat of the training action, and in cases like that you just need to raise your voice to draw your dog's attention back to you. Best you choose a combination of both methods.

Concerning Commands

You see, if you start training with a clicker and teach your dog tricks with it, there are more and more commands to be taught. As you know, your dog needs a command for every task, or he will get confused. Conversely, you will have to learn vocabulary. Write down every command and the task that goes with it. Otherwise, you might confuse them during the training. That's highly important, if you're not the only person responsible for the dog. Every member of the family who works with the dog must know the commands and what they stand for.

Especially, a puppy can get confused very easily and doesn't know how to combine command and task. That's, by the way, one of the major reasons, why there are dogs that obey to the commands of one person only and won't obey to the commands of other family members. The reason being they use the wrong words. Have you ever thought about it?

Here's an example from my own personal experience: "Drop" means for the dog to release something or spit something out, whereas I use the "No" command whenever he's barking at another dog without any reason. My husband uses the "Drop" command for everything the dog's not supposed to do. When Felix and my husband are coming back home from their walks, I would see my husband completely stressed because the dog didn't want to execute his commands again. Inquiring what happened, he would tell me, like so often, that Felix barked at other dogs and just didn't want to stop it. And my husband is at a loss to understand how I can manage to make our dog stop barking within seconds. Inquiring further into the matter and asking my husband which command he finally gave to the dog; his answer would usually be: "Drop". I don't know how many times I've told him that Felix wouldn't stop barking on the "Drop" command. On the contrary, the dog is further stressed by the fact that he's completely at a loss to know what he's supposed to spit out of his empty mouth. The two's got a communication problem because my husband never really took interest in the commands Felix was taught for the tasks. For him there is only "Sit", "Down", "Come", "Drop". Felix has got a much broader repertoire of words than that, but dog education has been "my project alone" from the very beginning, as my husband used to describe it. So, in the end I've come to educate a little man that dances to my piping - and that's not bad for me at all!

You can see from this example that you always have to act in concert like when educating a child or it's getting difficult to train your dog effectively.

Learning never ends!

There are dog-owners who really think that if their dogs know the basic commands, that would be it. Now, education is over, their dog is ready, and they don't have to take care of further dog-training. Far from it! You should never make that mistake. Of course, your dog will be well-behaved and comply with the "Sit" and "Down" commands, since you will demand them of him many times a day.

But it's a fact that sooner or later mistakes will be cropping up, if you don't continue your exercise-aimed training and don't stop correcting your dog whenever necessary. Your dog's head wants to be kept busy, and these exercises keep him busy and, apart from that, serve the purpose to teach him something new. Even if you've got a senior dog, he will be fit enough for at least some training exercises. Well, of course, the timeframe will be shorter and there will be exercises that you shouldn't do because of your dog's frailty. But, in any case, he will still be enjoying your training together.

Rehearse the basics again and again and rehearse them daily, and, if you wish, extend the exercises. Release your dog from the "Sit" position in order to have him retrieved something, or command him to execute a roll-out of the "Down" position. There are many possibilities to challenge and further the abilities of your dog.

Dogs that have never had any basic education often end up in animal shelters. Then, the new owners get themselves a grown-up dog that knows not a single command. You can teach commands to a grown-up dog, no problem, but it takes time for them to know and master them. During that time, you've got an uneducated dog in your house that has no manners whatsoever. I don't want to put a mark on every dog here, but there are animal shelter dogs that are quite well-behaved except for the fact that they haven't got a clue about "Sit" and "Down" and all that. For you it means you've got more work to teach your dog a certain basic behaviour.

As said, even the senior dog is willing to learn new things, only that he hasn't got that certain vigour anymore that a puppy is known for. For a puppy everything is a game, and everything is funny, and the fact alone that you're busy with him, is a great thing for him.

The exercises are a kind of game for him. The adult dog, on the other hand, can be attentive, but he soon shows a certain unwillingness to do the exercises and comply with your commands. That's why I recommend starting off early and stay on the ball.

Dog School – yes or no?

Opinions often diverge on the "dog school" subject, some dog-owners are euphoric about them, while others consider them completely stupid. I've made my experiences with different dog schools and have to say that my personal option is divergent, too. Generally speaking, I'm not against dog schools.

It all depends on the methods the dog schools employ. Puppy schools are great, in my opinion. The little rascal can be socialized as he can play and romp about with other puppies and give all he's got. I can really recommend a puppy school, since normally you won't meet other puppies on your daily walks, and living in the city, you don't have the chance to let your puppy play around with other young dogs. At least in our area, puppy schools usually have fenced-in grounds to prevent the little ones from escaping. Wrestling and bitching around is particularly important for puppies. What they learn there they learn for their life and in later times won't show behavioural problems towards their fellow dogs that often.

The dog school itself will help you to educate your dog. They usually work with larger groups, but there are dog schools that offer private lessons, if your dog can be easily distracted by others. There are also private lessons for problematic cases when, for example, the owners are at a loss to solve the problem and a trainer must assess the situation first. Inexperienced dog-owners profit from the dog school because they learn from scratch how to teach their dogs purposeful exercises and commands. But even experienced dog-owners like to go there because they simply appreciate the human togetherness and the fact that their dogs have always enough time to play with each other.

As said, I went to various dog schools, some of which I quite liked, while others I completely disliked. With my first dog, I went to a dog school whose dog trainer was very harsh and rough. He screamed a lot in the dog training ground, and the instructions he gave to the dog-owners were more like strict commands than nice and forthcoming tips. If a dog didn't want to understand his exercise, he would sometimes even intervene personally and pull violently at his leash or shout directly at him. I took two hours before I openly told him what I thought about all that. And I never went back there again. Such a behaviour is a no-go, and I never wanted to demand something like that from my dog.

Other dog schools, on the other hand, I considered to be just very pleasant places. The training personnel was friendly and helpful and always watchful, if I made a mistake during the exercises. If I made one, they advised me how to do it correctly. And they were always friendly to the dogs and the whole atmosphere was very pleasant.

As you see, the quality of dog schools differs a lot. That's why I'm far from condemning dog schools in general. You just have to be lucky finding the right school in your area, and you as far as the training is concerned, you may have to test several of these schools and go for trial runs. All that counts is that you're feeling at ease down there and that your dog can be completely relaxed.

As we originally come from a big city, I have to confess that I stopped my dog school activities fairly soon again. It was simply really expensive. If you're consistent in what you do and if you are prepared to invest enough time, you can educate your dog yourself. No problem. Now we live in the countryside and the dog schools are much cheaper out here, even if the choice of schools is rather limited. Unfortunately, they've got a long waiting list, but we've registered already. I'd like to see that school in any case. They offer playing hours for senior dogs which would be ideal for our Felix.

So, if it comes to dog schools, I can't offer you a definite "yes" or "no". The end of the day, it's all up to you what you do and if you want to go to a dog school with your dog or not.

Can I Overstrain the Puppy?

Your puppy might have fun exercising with you, but he hasn't yet got the kind of vigour and perseverance of a grown-up dog. His mind can be overstrained rather quickly, and that's why you should watch him closely. If he shows certain behavioural signs like yawning or is he doing his exercises in a sloppy manner, he is no longer attentive. So, keep your training units short, that means, three repetitions per exercise, then a break. That training structure would be perfect.

The break should take several hours. If you can arrange it, do a few exercises in the morning and then continue after lunch. Make sure your puppy had a relaxing time before you start your exercises and that he's done his business outside. Prior to your training, offer him small meals only. After too much food, he will be tired. Also, you will have difficulty in luring him with a treat because he's had enough to eat.

You can do your daily exercises first and then have a good playing time together. But playing time should never be prior to your exercises. Otherwise, puppies might be too excited to concentrate on something else. Also, some dogs tend to exhaust themselves to a degree that they are absolutely tired afterward. Your puppy's day means sleeping and snoozing quite a lot. Watch him: First he would be playing and romping about, then lying down and falling asleep again. These rest periods are very important for your puppy, since his mind is working at full speed. He must learn and discover so many new things, everything's smelling interesting and needs to be examined more closely. During sleep, his mind has got the time to process all the new impressions.

That's why it's hardly advisable to wake up a sleeping dog after the motto: "Now, I've got time, now we can exercise." Always consider the needs of your dog first, or the training will end up in frustration for you, and none of you will be having fun.

That's the reason why I mentioned earlier that you should try to find quiet surroundings for your training. If you go into a park where there are so many impressions and noises waiting for your puppy, he will have difficulty concentrating on the exercises. The same applies to kids playing in the same room you're doing your exercises. How shall this little dog be able to concentrate, if it's his wish to play with the kids? If your dog is older, distractions aren't such a matter of importance anymore. But anyway, there are dogs that can be easily distracted by environmental impressions. Some dogs wish to be right in the middle of the action. To make such a dog pay attention to you and your exercises, is a difficult task, you can be sure. So, it somehow depends on the character of your dog you always have to consider.

Your Puppy, Kids and other Pets

If you have kids or other pets, a puppy that's moving in can cause a lot of unrest, but also contribute to many great funny moments.

We always had cats in our house, but the way of living together with cats would differ from dog to dog. Our tomcat was a big and heavy animal with basically a really kind soul. Our daughter could do everything with him she wanted, and only in extreme cases he would protest against it. But when our first dog moved in, he didn't find things funny anymore. Though the little puppy didn't even have half the weight of the tomcat, he signalled him by hissing who would be in charge in the house. He made his stance clear, and they had no trouble with each other anymore. The puppy submitted, and both cat and dog lived together peacefully. Only the food bowls had separate locations because their jealousy about food was tremendous.

Our tomcat was to survive Bernie, our first dog, and we had great concerns about how it would work with a new dog. Felix, the little Chi, was a real dwarf when he moved into our house, but our tomcat welcomed him with open paws. He went up to him straight away, sniffed at him and showed no aversion whatsoever. The two of them would even play together and sleep in the same basket. It's astonishing to see how important something like affection can be. While our tomcat and Bernie just lived next to one another, a real friendship developed between the tomcat and Felix, a friendship that even outlasted the food bowl. Yes, I know, many dog-owner will start complaining now, but cat and dog can swap their food and have no problems. And they both ate from the bowl which, obviously, had the tastier contents.

When our tomcat died, Felix searched for him a long time. Something was missing. His friend was gone. We tried a foster dog for some time, but Felix didn't like him and there was trouble all the time. The right order of rank couldn't be established. But the foster dog could be placed somewhere else quite easily, so the two didn't get into real trouble. In autumn a cat came straying into our house that, obviously, had no owner, and she kept returning to us. We decided to keep her, and, as a matter of fact, the combination worked perfectly from the first minute. Cat and dog were friends and Felix seemed to get more lively again.

Both dogs, however, had no trouble whatsoever with the kids. Well, we only had to remind our daughter more than once that she shouldn't always annoy and upset the puppy because he would be in need of his resting time. Our first dog was a real kid-lover, whereas our dog now is rather mistrustful of them.

As you can see, it works - but it can get rather turbulent. Well, the moment your puppy is moving in is the moment you see, if things develop harmoniously or not. He needs a good start into the new family, and your kids have to be instructed by you what they are allowed to do and what they are not allowed to do. As far as other pets are concerned, the puppy is, by nature, relatively neutral. Everything is interesting and funny. It's up to you to see that his start works smoothly, particularly, should you be owner of a cat. A puppy notices when he's being scratched or hissed at a lot, so it might happen he develops an aversion to cats in general after a while.

As far as this subject is concerned, let's get into details now.

The Puppy and Kids

Kids and dogs are a great combination, and most puppies love kids. However, you should never generalize that. There are also insecure puppies that are afraid of toddlers and kids. So it's up to you again to make kids and dog get together. If your kid is old enough, you should talk about it and what a dog in the house would mean.

Of course, everybody is happy with a dog, but your kid needs to understand that responsibility is an important factor when having a pet. But always bear in mind: Even if you got yourself a dog because of your kids, it's you who's in charge and responsible! Never pass your responsibility on to your kids, they aren't able yet to know the whole extent of it. That's why it's in your hands to educate the puppy.

There isn't "the one" breed that you might call a "dog for kids". It always depends on the dog's individual character. As said, I have seen Golden Retrievers that were afraid of kids. So, it's all-important not to pick the dog breed on the basis of its look, but consider primarily its natural behavioural patterns. That's why many dog breeders offer get-to-know-days when you can bring your kids, and it's up to you to find out which of the puppies is interested in them. These get-to-know-days are also deemed important by animal shelters because the dog's supposed to stay in your family for all of his life. It would be a horrible fate for a dog, if you had to return him to the animal shelter just because he can't get along with your kids.

Your kid must learn and accept that the dog is not to be annoyed, upset, nor bossed around at will. If he knows his first commands, it's funny for a kid to let the dog playfully execute the commands over and over again. But your dog only ends up being listless and unwilling and might even refuse to comply with them later.

His sleeping place is a no-go area for the kids. That's the place where he can withdraw when he needs to relax. Everybody in the family have to accept that. If your kids are still small, they won't probably understand that. In such a case you should set up the dog place in a room where the kids normally have no access to, for example, in a corner in your bedroom or somewhere in the lobby.

Older kids like playing with dogs, but there are certain risks connected with it. Only allow them to play games in which they have got the dominating role. It might be difficult in the case of smaller kids and a bigger dog breed, but it's very important to pay good attention to it. If the kids are subordinate to the dog, he will soon realize that he can dominate them. It also means that he could do that at a later date when considering himself higher in rank than the kids. In case of doubt, just try to be present when your kids are playing with the dog. And intervene whenever you see that the dog's stronger than the kids.

Never let your kids walk the dog alone. Kids are not aware of the unpredictability of a dog, and they can end up in unpleasant and even dangerous situations. Always accompany your kids on their walks, so things are safe and secure. If your kids are older and in their teens, walking the dog alone shouldn't pose a problem anymore.

A good communication between kids and dogs is possible and eventually they even become friends. It's always nice to see how the three of them are snuggling on the floor, or the dog is joyously watching the two playing in the garden. If he's allowed to play with them and chase the ball, you realize just what a great team the three of them are.

Needless to say, it takes some time, and, sometimes, we have to slow down our son. As a toddler he isn't aware of many things, and sometimes he's a bit too rough for a little Chihuahua.

Have you ever wondered why puppies love kids so much? Perhaps it's their natural predisposition and character, being so clumsy and playful. Perhaps it's because they have got the unique chance to play the favourite game of a puppy without a break, while adults like us finish the game sooner or later. I'm not quite sure what it is, but it's simply so nice to see it happen.

Let me add something briefly at this point: I take the view that a dog has nothing to do whatsoever in the children's room. In our house the doors to these rooms are latticed, so the dog must stay out. There are always very small toys and parts of toys scattered about in the children's room, and when our dog was still a puppy, he really swallowed up one of them. Well, it came out again the natural way, but since then our dog has no business in the children's room anymore. Puppies are like small kids, and they have to try everything by taking it in their mouth and chew on it. And that's not only breaking toys, but it may lead to swallowing up parts of them. Apart from that, the kids allow the dog on their bed for snuggling. Here we've got the same problem: How is the dog supposed to know that he's allowed to do it in the children's room, but not allowed to do it in the parents' bedroom? That's difficult, and therefore the problem is sidestepped.

How Puppies get used to Pets

Should you have other pets already, the new one can cause problems. Well, of course, it depends on the animals that are in your house. Basically, another dog or another cat are to be considered the greatest of all challenges. If you've got small animals, your puppy must learn to leave them alone, something which in the case of hunting dog breeds would require you to stay absolutely consistent and resolute in your training practice.

In case of another dog: Ideally and if you go to see the puppy, you can take your dog with you. But it doesn't work in every case, and some dog breeders don't like to see strange dogs in their compounds. People in animal shelters, on the contrary, do appreciate that to ensure a peaceful get-to-know-day. If you can't take your dog with you or if you don't want to, bring the blanket of your dog and let the puppy play around with it for a while or lie down on it. Then, you give that blanket back to your dog, so he can absorb the puppy's smell.

The get-together that takes place at a later date will have to be done with much consideration. But it's also up to the dog himself how things can work out. If he's friendly towards strange dogs, you may introduce the two of them out on the street or in front of the house. If it works, you can enter your house together with the two dogs. That's highly important because if you bring the puppy into the house first, your dog might consider that an intrusion into his territory and react aggressively. Then watch how your dog's behaving before you decide to place the puppy on the ground. Best you start off in a room where the puppy can some first impressions of his new home. But watch out! Don't let the puppy come close to the sleeping or eating place of your dog. The ground on which the puppy is should be relatively neutral. If your dog's still remaining quiet and if he shows some first interest in the puppy, let them get to know each other.

But should your dog react by showing his natural territorial behaviour, you have to watch the situation carefully. In most cases, however, dogs just put the newcomers in check and show them who's been living in this house so far. Should your dog become aggressive and attack the puppy, separate both dogs for the sake of the puppy. In such an extreme case, I would even suggest getting the help of a professional dog trainer. He will be able to assess the situation objectively and give you advice what to do next.

In case of a cat: Well, that can be quite thrilling and can work out well from the very beginning or not, as I told you about our first dog. You have to know that, generally speaking, cats and dogs have different body languages and communication doesn't work so well in most cases.

As is a usual behaviour among them, dogs sniff at the bottoms of their fellow-dogs, whereas cats don't like that so much. So there can be first problems between cat and dog while they're coming closer to each other. The cat may make abundantly clear to the dog that she doesn't want to be sniffed at in the bottom. If the puppy is smaller than the cat, the boundaries are probably soon clarified. But should the dog be larger than the cat, it may happen that he wouldn't put up with what the cat's doing or that he would simply jump on her in a playful mood.

It's not a bad thing, should the cat extend her claws now and then because it helps the puppy to learn to know his boundaries. But be watchful! The cat should never hit him in the face, she could hurt his eyes. Compared to dogs, cats do have the home advantage: They can escape a situation by climbing up their scratch tree or a cupboard. These are good options for the cat to have a quiet place for observing the situation from above. Most cats like to be in an elevated position anyway. But even the biggest diva will soon accept that the family's got a new member. If they become the best of friends, can't be foreseen. Perhaps they simply condone themselves and decide to better avoid each other.

In order to prevent your cat from having the feeling to be second in line, see that her food and drink bowl is located apart from the one for the dog. The dog, on the other hand, shouldn't be able to get close to the cat toilet, so she can have her peace there. So, in the beginning you might have to rearrange certain things a bit. It's recommendable to separate cat and dog spatially, in case you're out of house or during the night. You may avoid trouble. But even if your cat can't jump on the dog like a tiger, there can be situations in which your puppy would definitely not be on the winning side.

They're equipped all those rooms where the dog has no business when being alone at home with a door lattice. He can move freely in the living room, in the lobby and the kitchen. However, bathroom, bedroom and children's room are only accessible for him, if somebody else is there. The door lattice has the advantage that the cat can jump over it, which made it possible that both avoid each other, and the dog leaves the cat alone when we're out. It was highly functional because the puppy would joyfully jump up and down on the cat when she wanted to find some rest in her basket. Looked funny but had the effect that the cat got a bushy tail only when seeing the puppy, though she liked him very much. But it's not very different the other way round: If the puppy wants to sleep and the cat is treading on him, he will get stressed sooner or later because of the lack of rest.

It's highly important to schedule times for playing and snuggling with your cat. I know that's quite hard since cats used to come to you when they feel like it - at least our cat. But it's important for the animal to experience that there is still affection for her. If you forget about her because your puppy is soaking up your time, she will take it amiss and might take her anger out on the dog. She simply needs more of your attention now. If she comes to you when you're not being occupied with the puppy, always treat her as a beloved part of your family.

As said before, some cats sound quite dangerous. They hiss, growl, and you might get the felling they're about to tear the dog to pieces. Don't panic! It won't happen. These little divas are just morose and show it openly. But things will become normal again, and the harmonious family life will be restored soon enough.

If you get yourself a shelter dog, you should in any case inquire if he's compatible with cats. The shelter people try everything to find out as much as possible about the dogs. There are animal shelters that offer customers to take the dog home after the first get-to-know day and to test the compatibility with the cat. Problem being you just can't find that out on one afternoon. So, it's best you inquire first, if the dog in question is compatible with cats or not.

I once had a shelter dog at home that had to be placed somewhere else eventually. Anyway, it was a really cute wire-haired Dachshund that we would have loved to adopt. However, people didn't know much about him, since his female dog-owner had died. The dog proved to be difficult, he neither liked closed doors nor would he like to suffer the lights turned out in our house during the night. Apart from that, he was averse to males. As soon as my husband came closer to me, he would start growling at him. Also, he used to avoid my husband in the house. Our tomcat was on day-release and, in summer, would be home only sporadically for getting his food. The Dachshund had been with us for three days and hadn't met our tomcat. On this day, however, when the dog was lying under the table, our tomcat strolled into the kitchen, not knowing about the dog. When the dog saw the cat, he immediately attacked her with arched chaps. The tomcat was faster, but now his fighting spirit had been aroused. From that time onward he would be roaming the house and whenever he was down on the ground, he would be attacked by the Dachshund. Spatial separation wasn't feasible because the dog didn't like closed doors, and we lived in a rental apartment at that time. On the other hand, we couldn't let him bark and yelp all the time. Well, the end of the story was that we brought him to a good friend of ours after a week. She had a foster home for shelter animals, too. It was a pity, I can say, we would have liked to adopt the dog. But in this case, reason had made the decision because our tomcat had the absolute privilege in our house. Apart from that, the situation with my husband had been quite deadlocked.

As you can see, the story with a shelter animal can go mighty wrong. That's why you should inform yourself in detail on the dog in question and prior to your decision to adopt him. Otherwise, it's heart-breaking for the dog - and for you as well -, if you have to return him to the shelter. That should never happen. The only consoling thought I had after our Dachshund story was that we only had a foster home as the animal shelter was overcrowded. Basically, the dog was supposed to be placed somewhere, and until then, we wanted to offer him a nice home.

In case of other pets: Well, I can speak from my own experience here as well. As an animal-loving home, we also have guinea pigs. Apart from the natural play instinct, both our dogs had no problem with them in the beginning. The dogs would euphorically stand in front of the cage and wanted to be part of the game. Well, our Chi, I have to admit, is really part of the game. He would climb through the little cage door when open and lie down next to the guinea pigs. Just to note it here. However, you should never do that with a big dog, there is acute danger that he might be hurting the rodents. But the dogs' interest in the guinea pets was too strong that they would stand barking in front of the cage one day and shake the cage with their claws. They should not behave like that, and it should be strictly forbidden. It isn't only bothersome, but the pets will be frightened. Moreover, granting this behaviour would mean to allow your dog to live out his hunting instinct.

If you realize that your dog starts getting noisy by the cage, distract him and give him the command to stop it. If he stops, praise him for complying and give him a treat. You will have to repeat this exercise several times before your dog's got it.

Should be keep the other pets in a garden shelter and your dog has access to it, make sure the shelter is well-secured and safe. A usual pet shelter can be easily overturned by a bigger dog. Make sure it has a really secure standing, so the dog won't be able to cause any damage to it. Needless to say, you must not allow your dog to stand barking in front of the garden shelter.

If your hares or guinea pigs can move about freely inside your house, the room should be locked. No dogs allowed there! These little animals can easily arouse the hunting instinct in your dog and a bigger dog is capable of hurting them seriously or, in case, even killing them. Our two dogs were only admitted to the pet room when I was present. And, as puppies, they became used to the animals very quickly. Never did one of our dogs even attempt to hunt the little animals and, in the end of the day, they would often even lie peacefully together on the ground.

That's the classic example of how it should be. But I don't mean to state that it always works that way. Bear in mind that my two dogs were themselves little animals when they were puppies. The Chi wasn't much larger in size than a guinea pig, and the mixed-breed was about six weeks old when he moved into our home. So, he was very small, too.

Let me briefly note here: I know that the mixed-breed was much too young. But he was already bottle-fed by the breeder, since the litter with eight puppies was big and the mother-dog didn't want to accept the last one of them. The breeder had to put him to his mother's teats to ensure he's being milk-fed at all. Since he didn't want to spare the effort to bottle-feed the dog day after day himself, he decided to give him away as soon as possible. That's why we got him quite early. But actually, that doesn't matter in this present context.

As said elsewhere, I don't recommend you allow a dog with a distinct hunting instinct or a bigger breed puppy to be together with small pets. It can go mighty wrong. Basically, there is no problem with that, and it won't take that long for most dogs to accept animals living in a cage, should they be used to them from puppy age.

If you're getting yourself a shelter dog, you have to test, if it works. In case of doubt, the cage has to be placed in a locked-up room or, at least, be located in an elevated position, for example on a table. It always depends on the dog. Some dogs wouldn't be interested in the pets at all, while others would go mad seeing them. Your advantage here is that it's up to you to actively avoid dog and pets getting together. But always bear in mind that the little dwellers are stuck inside a cage.

In the end, your personal patience will prove it right and also that you allow your dog to get used to the new little friends. Don't expect too much and, above all, don't expect great friendships between your dog and the other pets. Only the relationship between your dog and your kids must as a rule be working smoothly. If you've got a puppy, that won't be much of a problem because he will learn to accept them in no time.

How to Understand the Language of Dogs

If amateur or well-experienced dog-owner, to understand the language of a dog, isn't always that simple. He mainly communicates with you by means of gestures, facial expressions and posture. Of course, he can give mouth. But when communicating with you, that's not the rule. That's why many people misunderstand dogs so often.

Many amateurs think a dog is friendly and in good mood when wagging his tail. But they usually don't take notice of the way the dog's holding his tail - many people simply don't know that they have to pay attention to that. So, people's life together with dogs can be spoiled by these basic misunderstandings.

If you have kids, teach them what the dog is communicating when, for example, his tail is clamped between his hind legs. It's very important for kids they are understanding the language of the dog. They should be able to notice, if the dog's afraid of something or if he wishes to be left alone. A kid who can read the body language of the dog might not be in danger to be bitten by a strange dog when touching him. Generally speaking, a kid shouldn't do that, but, unfortunately enough, it happens much too often. Kids who are raised together with a dog often see a big cuddly bear in him that just wants to be caressed all the time. But there are many dogs in the parks that don't really like kids, and at the other end of the leash there are often dog-owners who don't care much how the dog is reacting. Always remember what I said above about him, "that just wants to play". If a dog fetches, the blame would be on the kid because "my dog has never done something like that before". If I really think about it, there are so many statements by dog-owners that make abundantly clear that they have no clue whatsoever about the own dog. What a pity it is!

Well, how's your do communicate with you? There are acoustic signals like barking or yelping or others. Dogs mainly use them when being with their fellows. Some dogs, however, would give such signals when having lost visual contact with their human. You can judge from the barking, if it's an aggressive sound or rather a "Hey, I want something from your food on the table" - that's a more demanding barking.

As far as gestures are concerned, your dog would use his tail and his ears. You can judge from their position, if your dog is in a positive mood, frightened or attentive. More about that presently.

Then, there is the facial expression as part of the language of the dogs. Well, dogs are masters if it comes to that. The eyes play the main role. Perhaps you have experienced how hard it is to resist the innocent look of a Dachshund. My dog, for example, is absolutely prof in looking like suffering, if he's bugged by something. This summer, he had an ant between the pads of his paw. In its panic this little ant was defending itself, and, as we all know, that's quite a burning sensation. The poor dog was able to walk on three legs only and was suffering from "terrible pain" for three hours. Well, the glance he gave me was priceless. Don't get me wrong on this. If my dog's got pain, it's not funny at all. But if he's really sick, he would withdraw into his basket and wants to be left alone. Felix, however, is big into the drama and knows exactly which buttons he must press to get nursed a bit. As said, it was only a single ant, and more or less everybody of us has been in contact with these little crawling insects. So, it's not that bad. In any case - that's for facial expression. Most dogs simply know how to give that glance.

Posture is another aspect of the language of the dogs and is expressive of their mood. Many dog-owners, however, don't care much about it. If you watch your dog a bit more closely, you can literally read many of his postures.

Dogs communicate via scents. Well, it's not that interesting for humans like us because we can't read them. But it's highly informing for other dogs. That's why you should give your male dog time to place his scent marks on your daily round. He must do that, and if you don't let him do it, he will get frustrated. However, when doing your exercises, it's you who's in the focus of his attention. During the training, he should neither be reading scent marks nor placing them. He can do it later after your exercises.

But you should make the mistake to wait for such signals from your dogs. Communication is a combination of these aspects. Always watch your dog, which extremities and parts of his body are used in which way. Watch his posture and listen attentively to the sounds he's making.

Your dog doesn't communicate with one extremity only, but with his entire body. And it's your task to recognize the elements and understand the combination. Be sure, many times you will get it wrong. That can happen even to me sometimes.

Communicating with the Tail

Your dog does talk a lot with his tail, it's his antenna to the outside world. He can show and express the whole repertoire of his feelings with it. His entire rear part is shaking, when your dog is wagging his tail happily. You know that already. Looks funny when trying to walk at the same time, as you might get the impression he's going to tumble over the next moment.

But here's the downside of it. Even when wagging his tail, your dog must not be in a happy mood. Basically, the tail is expressive of all states of possible excitement, that means, also of aggression.

If your four-legged friend is keeping his tail down, it is meant to communicate that he's content and balanced. His tail doesn't need to be wagging fast. No, it's moving all slowly and timidly. If your dog is holding it up high, he's absolutely focussed. He shows you that something has just aroused his interest, and he has to look attentively what it might be. If your dog clamps his tail between his hind legs, he's afraid of something. In such a moment, he may also suddenly bite. It's time for you now to be especially watchful and find out what he's afraid of.

My dog would clamp his tail when he's done something stupid. I came home once and wondered why he wasn't waiting for me at the door as usual. Upon calling him, he came up to me but hesitatingly, with his tail between his hind legs, his ears pulled back, and his head held to the side for the purpose of appeasement. His whole posture showed me that he had done something stupid and wanted to say sorry for it now. Well, it wasn't long before that I saw what it was. Obviously, he had the runs and made his business on the bathroom floor. Well, of course, no reason to scold him. Things like that are disposed of without any comment. In the end, it wasn't his fault and, lucky enough, it wasn't the carpet that was spoiled. His posture showed me that he was having a bad conscience and, perhaps, was even a little afraid of what might happen, if I see it. But dogs don't always communicate in such an extreme manner.

But you see that watching is the key to learning the language of your dog.

Communicating with the Ears

Well, what can I say? The ears can't move as eloquently as the tail. However, two positions are highly important to know: Cocked ears and backward-bent ears.

If your dog bends his ears backward, it's supposed to show you that he's submissive. You can almost say he's making himself smaller. If his ears are cocked, he's watchful and self-reliant. A dog with cocked ears could run after another dog or a biker the next moment. His ears assume the same position during your training units and when he's absolutely focused on you.

Now, some dogs have droopy ears which makes it more difficult for you to see, if his ears are cocked or not. Just look at the highest point of his ears - the ear root, and you will clearly see how your dog's ears are positioned. In some cases, the droopy ears of the dog can cock a bit, for example, when your dog's moving them up.

Demand

If your dog wants something from you, like for example play, he will demand you to do it, Some dogs may even bark, but not all of them. However, his body language is definite: a raised-up rear, elevated together with his tail, a lowered upper body and a wagging tail. Perhaps he's nudging you with his mouth or barking.

This is his way of showing you that he wants to play or go out. Even dance-like movements in front of you should be understood as a sign that he's in the playing mood.

But you shouldn't confuse this posture with relaxation. My Chi, for example, would be having this posture when he's been up for quite a long time. I presume it's meant to relieve his back. He would raise his rear while the front part of his body is being lowered. Sometimes lowered so much that he can put his head flat on the ground. His tail is not cocked but is hanging down in a relaxed manner. He's closing his eyes and dozes off until he's lying down with his whole body.

Barking

For your dog, barking is a means of communication that he will use for many purposes. In most cases he wants to stress something, if you don't want to understand him. That's his way of adding emphasis to his body language. So always watch his body language and facial expression when he's barking. You will be able to assess much more easily what he's trying to communicate.

There are different modes of barking, as it were. If you know your dog really well, you can judge from the sound of his barking what things are about.

There is a happy barking, a defensive barking, barking as a warning, a frustration barking and barking for fear. Besides, there is the so-called trained barking, which you might have taught your dog with a certain exercise.

The modes of barking differ in pitch and can be differentiated like his postures. Barking for fear produces a high pitch, whereas barking as a warning or defensive barking are rather low modes like the typical growling sound.

Since every dog has his own barking sound, you have to learn to differentiate between the modes and assess their meaning. I have heard many Chihuahuas bark with a very high pitch. But listening to it, you certainly recognize the barking sound of a smaller dog. The sound of my Chi, for example, can be likened to that of a medium-sized dog, so it's rather low. If you hear him, you won't expect a little Chi standing at the garden door.

Growling

This is a sound which is falsely interpreted by many amateurs. They think that if a dog's growling, he's menacing. However, that's not the case. As far as growling is concerned, it's likewise an expression of various moods and, like barking, also differs in pitch.

Apart from that, growling is understood as a sign of warning, which you should take seriously. Your dog is growling when he's not feeling at ease, being bothered or intending to express his despair. If he's driven into a corner, for example, he's growling and telling you: "Let me alone". If you comply with his wish, everything's fine. Unless it may happen that his growling is followed by a bite because he's at a loss to find another way out of the situation.

Teach that to your kids, too. A growling dog should always be left alone and never be touched. My Chi is growling when he's wrapping himself up in his blanket. So it's rather a contended growling that soon becomes a deep sigh and snoring in the end. For him, it's an expression of feeling at ease. It's no comparison to that kind of growling he gives when he feels being threatened by another dog. You can simply hear it.

Recognizing Signals of Appeasement

This behaviour is deeply rooted in your dog's nature and can be well observed when dogs are with their fellows. You can judge from that behaviour, if a dog has been well socialized, and he's communicating that with his body only. He shows you clearly that he intends to appease a conflict or to prevent it from happening. For example, when he's being attacked by a stronger dog. He will immediately take the appeasing posture, telling the other dog: "I'm submitting to you; I know that you're stronger. Let us part without fighting."

There are various appeasement signals your dog can use. But he can also express them all at once. As I mentioned above, such as my dog behaves, it's typical and thus easy to assess. Yet sometimes it can be misunderstood because the dog is giving but one signal.

Yawning, slow movements, turning away, and splitting are typical modes of the dogs' appeasement behaviour.

If your dog yawns, you probably think he's tired. But he isn't. Yawning is a means for calming himself in a stressful situation. My Chi, for example, would yawn, if he's allowed out in the garden. Until I put on shoes and coat, he's rushing up and down the hallway and tripping restlessly at the front door of our house. Doing so, he would yawn now and then. That shows me that he must calm himself down a bit because he's so agitated to be admitted to the garden.

But since yawning isn't that definite in meaning, it's your task to watch how your dog's generally behaving.

Your dog's realizing when you're in a hurry and stressed. He will calm you, and therefore, his movements are slower than usual. That, however, what may drive you nuts in your rush, is pure appeasement from the dog's point of view. Well, funny fact is, the more you urge him to be faster, the more slowly he gets.

An example: I overslept, and the kids should be sitting at the breakfast-table. I jump out of bed, into my pants and take the dog out. What is usually a matter of a short while, takes ages. The dog appears to be sneaking along. He's sniffing here and there and moves on absolutely sluggishly. He doesn't even think of lifting his leg and empty himself. Then, after a while, I tell him to be faster. Of course, that's pointless, he doesn't get me, but somehow, it seems to calm me. He takes care of his business here and there, and when I consider him to be ready, we would go home, but at a faster pace. But my dog is sneaking behind me, and that which drives me crazy is but a signal of appeasement for my Chi. He wants to tell me: "Slow down a bit and don't get stressed." We had that situation again some time ago. But having a look at my watch, I thought to myself: "That's ok, we're still in time." So, I calmed down a bit and slowed down. And lo and behold, all at once my dog continued on his way at a normal pace, like he would usually do.

Bear in mind, he isn't slow to show you that it's him that determines the pace. That's not a behaviour of dominance, he simply tries to slow you down.

If the dog wants to appease, he turns his back to you and tries to avoid meeting your glance. That can happen when another dog or another human is coming too close to him, and he's feeling uneasy. If you call your dog, he will come up to you because he knows that he's entitled to do so, but he will move very slowly and turning his head to the side.

Splitting is typical behaviour dogs would also show when they are with their kind. If you wish to embrace somebody, your dog might push himself between your legs. That's not a signal of jealousy, and it's not his intention to behave in a dominant way. He's pushing himself between your legs, since he wants to keep you apart from each other. For him, it's a signal of appeasement, since bodily nearness is considered to be potentially dangerous by your dog, and he would interfere to avert a fight. If several dogs are playing with each other, you can observe this behaviour, too. As soon as two dogs get in bodily touch, a third dog would interfere with the intention to avert a conflict and a fight.

Well, this behaviour is more than just bothersome in the human context, and, for example, if you wish to embrace the kids or your partner. But your dog would only follow his natural instincts and would do what is deeply rooted in his character. You can simply push him aside or ignore him. You can also command "Sit". Should his behaviour be too annoying, it can't be helped, your dog will have to leave the room when you're together with your partner.

Our Chi, for example, usually sleeps next to our bed and that works perfect. But as soon as my husband and me want to snuggle and are coming too close to each other, our dog may suddenly leap on the bed and pushing his body between us. He places himself right in the middle between us. If I command him back to his basket, he will move off, but return right away. What looks like he just wants to join you snuggling can be really bothersome, I tell you. He will definitely have to sleep in his basket in the living room on those nights.

Emotions of Dogs

There are people, you think that animals would have no emotions. That's absolute nonsense. If an animal would have no emotions, he wouldn't be able to learn, establish relationships and couldn't survive in the end. Scientists could find out that animals have emotions and are able to show these emotions. If you take the puppies away from a mother-dog, she will be sad and search for them. That's not only natural instincts, but these are also maternal feelings.

To make your dog feel at ease, you should always care for his emotions and try to deepen that relationship between the two of you. From my own experience, I can tell you, however, that the deeper the relationship is, the more painful it will be for you when it will end after many years together. This is perhaps a reason by there are dog-owners who want to see the animal as a guarding or working dog and try not to snuggle too much with the dog. But let's be honest. In such a case, I don't need a dog. There is nothing like the look your dog has for you when you're coming home. This pure joy in his eyes. Or those contented sighs when you are tickling his favourite spot.

How else could it be: If your dog's happy or not, you can see from his body language. It should be the objective of every dog-owner to have a happy dog. If that's the case, you can clearly judge from the language of his body.

If he's happy, his eyes will be gently and lightly focussed on a target. His brow will be relaxed, the ears loose and casually hanging down, or his droopy ears will be lightly moved when he's walking. Even if your dog can't smile, you will have the feeling that he's doing it anyway because his facial expressions are absolutely relaxed. He may have opened his lips a chink and his tongue may be hanging out calmly. His tail will be wagging lightly in the middle of his body, and in case it's wagging profusely, the entire rear part of his body will be shaking, too.

That's about how your dog's looking when he's absolutely happy and pleased. Have a closer at him. Another nice sign when he's feeling well: He's rolling his body around to lie on his back, holding his head sideways and stretching out his legs. This gesture, however, can be misinterpreted. If your dog wants to submit himself, he will also lie down, turn around on his back and show you his belly. The reason being that the belly is the most vulnerable part of his body. In case of a brawl, the weaker one would submit himself to the stronger on in this manner. It's his way to show that he's submissive. With his belly up, the weaker dog could be hurt seriously by the stronger dog without difficulty.

As soon as your dog's afraid of something, his body language is harder to assess. In such a situation, no dog will react like others. That's why you should focus on that subject, find out about the typical signs of fear and be able to recognize them with your dog. A puppy that's afraid of something would typically excrete droppings or release urine. Don't scold the dog for that. It's his nature. Literally speaking, he will have defecated into his trousers.

There are further signs to be observed: Ducking away, trembling, standing like paralyzed or running away. His tail will be motionless, hanging down or being completely clamped between his hind legs. The lips of your dog will appear to be tense. There are dogs that are incessantly licking their lips or are yawning. His brow will be troubled, and head and body will be lowered or falling forward. His ears will be all flat at his head that is lowered and turned to the side. If you look him in the eyes, they will be widened and rigid for fear. They may also be twitching fast or squinting. You see? This is exactly the picture I had when he excreted his droppings in the kitchen.

It should have foremost priority for you not to scold your dog for his fear. Talk to him in a calm manner and find out the reason of his fear. But be cautious! You can show him that you're there for him. But, please, don't overdo it. Your nearness is not supposed to be a kind of reward for him because he might get the impression that he's being praised for something he's afraid of. And the problem might pop up again and again.

Let's come to dogs that are aggressive - which is, unfortunately enough, not so rare a case. Even if it's your dog and you know him, be careful. In some cases, a dog that's aggressive might even bite his owner.

Right at the start, your dog is showing you that something is bugging him. Though being quiet, he's growling. That when he's not really aggressive yet. He just wants to warn you. If nothing happens, he can get really berserk. He opens his mouth while arching his lips. His eyes assume an adamantine expression and are fixing you without blinking. The brow is troubled, and his ears can be all flat at his head, while the fur of his neck and his back is standing on end to appear higher and more menacing. His tail will be motionless, since all of his body weight will be concentrated on his fore paws in order to be ready to rush forward for attack.

If that's the way your dog behaves, I advise you to hold the leash short and with full grip. Also, try to distract the dog to get him out of the attack mode. Talk to him in a very calm manner and don't shout at him. That would only heat up his aggression all the more.

Now, there are dogs that are frustrated for quite different reasons. Various incidents can cause these frustrations. However, it can also be long-term and cause some kind of depressive mood. But why could your dog be frustrated? He might love to have something and won't get it, like for example a toy. Perhaps he feels the urge to go outside and you're not reacting. There are situations that can be unpleasant for a dog, can be the reason for frustration, all the more, if this particular situation happens again and again.

If your dog's frustrated, he's tense and his legs are stiffened, while he might be barking all day long or withdraw himself. Perhaps it might be hard to distract him because he's all fixed on the subject of his frustration. His eyes will be opened wide and unblinking; his ears will be arched high. If he doesn't bark, his lips appear stiff, and the corners of his mouth will be pushed forward.

This state won't last, your dog will give up sooner or later and accept the facts as they are. That, however, can lead into some kind of depression, if these facts are repetitive. Now, it's all-important to show him the deepest of your affection and help him to calm down. But, in any case, try to find the reasons for his frustration and resolve matters.

Your dog will be relieved when he's overcome his fears. You will be able to see physically how these fears literally fall off his entire body. Suddenly, his eyes will turn gentle, his ears will be relaxed again, and your dog will appear soft and happily relieved. Some dogs would start yawning in such a situation. If your dog is rather quiet, he will probably lower his head and stay quiet, whereas a lively dog starts running and stretching out the whole of his body.

Assign a task to your dog, and you will see how his mind starts working, and he will focus on it. As a matter of fact, you can read the language of his body quite well. His eyes are round and clear, and he's looking attentively on the object or on you. His ears are pointed and tilted forward, his mouth is shut or slightly opened so that his tongue can be seen. His head is being held up high, and if you show him something in the distance, he will stretch his head into that direction. His tail is standing up and either motionless or moving.

Probably your head's spinning right now, but fact is: It's not always that easy to catch the situation as I described it above. From his eyes and his facial expression alone, you're able to ascertain how your dog's feeling. Don't expect him to be always happy and pleased. That's unrealistic. There will always be situations unpleasant for him, causing fear or making him angry. Just like a little kid, he will try to get his own way and be frustrated in case of failure. You will give your best for your dog to have a nice life, but always remember: You've got bad days or bad moments yourself, and it's your dog's natural right to have them, too. A balanced dog is capable of coping with these emotions and become calm again. As usual, it's important for you personally to stay calm and relaxed. Don't scream at him or scold him. It makes no sense because the only thing that will happen is that his mood is worsening and that it won't be easier for him to calm down again.

Emergency Tips in Case of Problems

Even the best of educations can go wrong. Why and in what direction can't be generally said. It often happens when the dog's in his teens and he would try to act out his will. But also grown-up dogs can suddenly do strange things. Sometimes the dog may not get enough affection. Of course, he gets his food, can go out, gets his cuddles, but perhaps you haven't got enough time to play with him presently.

It's often these trifles that can get your dog, a creature of habit, out of his grind, and things stop working like a clockwork.

I'm listing just a few problems that can crop up and which I've had the chance to experience myself. The two births of my kids, a new job, sudden changes in the daily walking routine as well as our moving into another home were noticeable turning-points for him. All that contributed to the fact that things wouldn't work out so well with the dog for some time. You should face these things emotionally and show understanding for the dog's changed situation. There has been a change in his life which he can't cope with so easily. But with your help he will finally make it and soon things will be running as smoothly as usual. Perhaps even better.

Sometimes, however, it's you who is to blame for the behaviour of the dog. Often, you simply lack that particular awareness for it, but always bear in mind that your dog's a very sensitive being. If you are too yielding, he will take over control. That's fact. There must be a leader in every pack, and if you humans can't do it, it's the dog's turn. That's how he thinks. Therefore, I always stress that it's all-important to stay consistent in all you do. My mixed-breed, for example, was a prof in taking over. Whenever he noticed that people were too compliant, he suddenly posed like the landlord and tried to stay away from things. The Chi, on the other hand, wouldn't abuse a situation in which you are less consistent and resolute. Luckily enough, I'm at a loss to say when exactly he would take over the position of the leader. I haven't been that inconsistent in my behaviour yet.

But now let's come to the typical problems every dog-owner will be faced with sooner or later:

The Dog isn't interested in you

That's not a problem you're faced with, should you have a puppy. Puppies are interested in everything, without exception. But when your dog's a bit older, it may happen quite easily, that he's not interested in you. You're calling him, and he just won't react to your command, let alone turn his glance into your direction. And only grudgingly he would even come for playing a game with you or will finish it very soon.

It almost seems he would be playing with you only to do you a favour. Somehow, you feel like being but a tiresome thing for him that he's forced to deal with, though he would very much like to do something else.

Well, if that happens, you're the problem. Sounds rude, but it's a fact. Think hard. You might pamper your dog too much. Is he being overwhelmed with your affection, and are the two of you together in an active and focussed manner every minute of the day? It might go without saying for you personally because you love your dog and want to be together with him all the time. But for your dog it's simply too much of everything. You're not so interesting for him anymore because you're with him every free minute of the day anyway.

It's a much better strategy to reserve special time for your dog and fill the moments together with high-quality activities: Intensive playing or snuggling, bonding walks or simply training exercises. But these activities should be restricted to a certain time during the day. Well, you take your time for other things, too. Your dog can be with you, though you can't pay so much attention to him, like for example, when cleaning the house or cooking in the kitchen. Always bear in mind, it's up to you to decide when there's time for the dog and for playing.

If your dog notices that he isn't always in the centre of interest, you give him the chance to renew his interest in your person. If you work with him, he'll be happy again. It will be the highlight of the day for him, all the more that he can't know yet what you're going to do with him. The fact alone that he's at a loss to know, if you're going to play together, do some exercises or whatever, is a reason for him to find you interesting. But, of course, always pick those activities that your dog is loving most.

I had the same problem with my mixed-breed. We were still without kids, and I actively spent every free minute with him. It was absolutely great for him, so what else could I have offered him? When I started to arrange separate dog times during the day, which would leave me enough time to do my daily things, it was hard to cope with for him in the beginning. He would follow me into every room, actively demanding my attention. He soon realized that I didn't react to his demands and so he withdrew into his basket. When I had finished my work and dog time had come, he was really happy again. Suddenly, he had a renewed interest in me and would comply with my commands when out for a walk.

Therefore, always be mindful of the necessity to dedicate special times to your dog. It might be difficult for you to arrange these times, but even if you have a job, a family, and a thousand things to do, it should be working.

He's defending his Toys

Though it's still a game for the puppy, teen or adult dogs would put all their powers into it - defending their toys. That's why it should be an early training for your puppy to learn that he's entitled to give his toys away, should you command him to. That works quite well with puppies in most cases, but all of a sudden, while growing up, your dog starts to defend his prey. As stressed in a precious chapter, he's not supposed to do that.

It's your task to train that behaviour with your dog again and again. That's why I keep saying that you have to do the exercises over and over again. If you wish, even at irregular intervals. But everything that your dog has been taught already, must be repeated to become part of his behavioural patterns.

So, if your dog doesn't want to share something any longer, don't take it from him violently. He will be growling, anyway, because he wants to warn you not to take away his toy. Take his favourite treat and offer him a deal: Toy for treat. Repeat that several times because he must learn that there's something much better in return for his toy.

If your dog starts defending his food, just re-do the exercise as described further above. Prepare his meet in front of him, so he can watch you. Say the "Sit" command before you put it on the ground for him. Then, you signal him that he's allowed to eat from his bowl.

If your dog is a grown-up and that trick doesn't work anymore, you can also consult a professional dog-trainer. He can assess the situation and give you valuable advice. There can be situations that defy troubleshooting because small things you don't think of might be going wrong. But the dog-trainer should be in the know how to solve the problems and let you know how to handle everything effectively.

Lucky us! We never had that problem with toys or food, as described above. Our dogs were taught when they were still puppies, and, actually, that particular exercise was repeated many times, I can tell. It was so important for me because of the kids. Well, you don't have your eyes everywhere, do you? Though both dogs were fed in the kitchen and the kitchen door was latticed, we never had these problems. The dog can quietly eat his food, and me, I can be certain that none of my kids would try to fetch a bite from his bowl. The Chi allows me to take his food, even when he's eating. However, if my husband or one of my kids want to steal a piece of his bread that fell off the table, he would defend it with growling and snarling noises. As far as that's concerned, you can clearly see who's the leader of the pack for him: Indubitably me.

The Dog is permanently distracted

This problem isn't that rare, particularly in case of younger dogs. He wants to play with every dog outside and is permanently looking into the direction of other dogs. It's very difficult to do your exercises with him because he's always distracted.

My advice is that you should reduce his contact with other dogs and teach him to pass by other dogs without getting in touch with them. If he successfully completed the exercise, you could give him a treat. This works only if your dog is walking on the leash and complies with your "Heel" command. But make sure the location of your training is quiet, which means other dogs should be passing by and playing all the time.

Mainly, this kind of problem is also based on a certain lack of interest for the owner, as mentioned above. So, you have to try to make yourself more interesting for the dog. As soon as he's done his exercises and is behaving well, you may let him play with the other dogs for some time. Here, we have another learning effect, namely that your dog notices that it's worth doing exercises with you because he allowed to play with the other dogs afterward.

Generally speaking, there are dogs that are can be easily distracted by different environmental factors, like street noise, playing kids. Even birds can be reason for his being distracted. Needless to say, you can't avoid all of these factors in daily life, though you can at least look for a quiet location for your dog training. It's important that your dog must find you more interesting than the sources of distraction. Think about the activities your dog loves most. If you pick the same exercises or the same schedule over and over again, it might be boring for him, so he can be distracted more easily. I mentioned it elsewhere that there are dog breeds that, for example, like hunting better than doing exercises. So, it can make sense to reduce the training exercises and do something the dog really loves to do instead, for example, retrieving, dog agility or whatever. Just get to know the interests and predilections of your dog.

The Dog is Unwilling to Comply

Marginally, this problem has got to do with disinterest in your person, too. You walk the dog, and he won't even think of turning around to see where you are or even coming up to you on call. Primarily, you should intensify this exercise in such a case, that is, do it again at home. If your dog's is well-behaved enough to come up to you when you call him, take a towline and go outside with him for further training. And when he's coming up to you, reward him with a treat.

The towline gives you a certain safety, that means, you can get the dog back in case he shouldn't comply to follow your call anymore. The trigger of this behaviour might be too much attention you're paying to your dog.

My mixed-breed revealed the same behaviour, but in his case it was triggered by the fact that he became hard of hearing and couldn't hear me anymore.

A dog-trainer once told me how he's doing this exercise to avoid having the long towline on him all the time. I don't like this method and don't want to recommend it. But I'd like to let you know about it here, so you're warned, should a dog trainer suggest the same to you one day. Its basis is to refuse to feed the dog and let him starve for two days. Then, you take his food outside and call the dog. If he's well-behaved enough to comply, you give him some food.

No question, the dog will come because he's hungry. However, I don't like the idea to bait the dog with food and let him starve to make him comply with the command. Everyone - animal or human - would come as fast as possible when hungry enough to eat a horse. Yet I strongly doubt that there is a genuine learning effect for the dog in all of that. When he's got his fill and going out with you afterward, there will be no more reason for him to react to your call. In my view, this is a kind of exercise that makes no real sense.

The Dog Finishes the Exercise

You're rehearsing with your dog and, suddenly, he's getting up out of the "Sit" position without your release command. It happens quite often that the dog would finish his exercise by himself. What might be the reason? In the beginning, the reason could be that he doesn't yet know how to do the exercise. However, it could be that you give him his treat the moment he's lying down. Wait a short while, so your "Stay" command can make sense for him. Could it be that you forget to finish the exercise sometimes? In such a case, the dog finishes it at will.

As you see, the reasons can be numerous. That's why you should ponder the possible reasons for this problem. A dog that has executed this exercise reliably in the past must have a real reason to finish it by himself.

Try to correct him when he's doing it. Send him back into the basic training position and wait a second before you give him his treat. Extend the timeframe steadily and give him his treat when he's getting up on your command. Please don't forget to finish an exercise yourself. If he's sitting, and you walk off without finishing it, it will make no sense whatsoever for the dog.

The father of a girlfriend of mine had a German Shepherd dog that he took to his job every day. He worked as a night watch; his dog was trained to attack and would absolutely comply with the commands of his owner. When visiting my girlfriend, he would be lying in the hallway where he was supposed to stay and wouldn't move an inch, even when being alone. He was called when there was feeding time. After that, he was sent back to his place. As a kid, I used to keep distance when passing him because, normally, he would start growling when I approached him. As said, he was perfectly trained and obeyed every word. In short, it was that kind of dog you could be really afraid of as a kid. I keep on wondering how my girl-friend's father could make it in the first place because even when he wasn't at home, the dog would be well-behaved enough to remain in his place. He didn't even try to get up or change his position in the meantime. He was lying "down" there and except for his eyes and his head, no part of his body would be moving an inch. Today, I sometimes wonder, if he wasn't drilled in a very rough and rude way. I say "drilled" intentionally, since until the present day, I've never met a dog that would remain absolutely motionless in his position for many hours.

Of course, this is a good example of how it shouldn't be. I mentioned it elsewhere that you should never leave the house after you gave your dog the "Down and Stay" command. Normally, your dog won't just do it, and you can't correct him because you're not at home. I mean to say: Rehearse again and again, and do it on a regular basis, correct him and never forget to finish all your exercises explicitly.

Trouble staying alone

If it worked so far, and isn't working anymore, try to find the reason. Perhaps, you recently left your dog alone for too long. Perhaps he's just bored.

Make sure the dog can romp about outside and empty himself before you leave home for some a longer time. Give him something to busy himself while you're not in, like his toy or a chewing bone. Ideally, you take him out for a big round because, afterward, he will be sleeping, and you can go out for, say three or four hours in a row.

Even if it might prove a bit difficult but leave your house and stay in the vicinity of the front door or a window for a short while. Wait how long it takes until he starts barking or yelping. This helps you to assess the length of time you can be out.

Your dog gets used to the fact that there's always somebody in the house, for example, if you've been together with him because you have been off work for some time or been sick. In such cases, you should try to schedule your dog's daily routine as sensible as possible. That means, for example, should you be in the office between 9 AM and 12 PM, try not to play with the dog, go out with him or be otherwise busy with him within that same period of time. If you're working home office, use a separate room the dog is not admitted to. His daily schedule shouldn't differ from his schedule when you're working in the office. He wouldn't understand that you're at home for a longer time and, theoretically, could do something together with him, while, then again, you're out during the same period of time. If you can be busy with your dog because you're sick and can't do anything else, try to make him get used to being alone again in due course. If you know, for example, that you have to go back to work after four weeks of sick leave, try to leave your dog alone, that is, extend the period daywise, so he can get accustomed to it.

My Chi, for example, is used to staying alone every day from 8 AM until 12 PM. In the beginning, I took him with me to the office, but only on certain days. It was no problem for him, and even today he's aware of the fact that he's supposed to do something on his own, though I'm working from home now. At 7:30 AM I usually take the kids to school, and, shortly before leaving the house, he would be back in his basket. After coming home around 8 AM, I sit down at my desk, while he would stay in his basket until 12 PM. Then, he would get up relaxed, drink some water, play with his ball, and around 12:20 PM he would be standing next to me signalling that it's time for his walk. As soon as we put on our coats or shoes and tell him to go to his place, he knows that he can't come with us this time and would be well-behaved enough to lie down in his basket.

Our mixed-breed was different in that respect. He was used to the fact that there was somebody in the house all the time. My husband was doing shifts at that time, and it happened only a few times that the dog had to stay alone all late morning. During that time, he wouldn't bark or yelp, but would do a lot of other stupid things, like emptying trash bins, rummaging through shelves or biting shoes, if he's got the chance to get hold of them. He didn't like being alone, and you could see it on his face how sad he became when he realized that he can't come with us.

That made me understand the big difference, if a dog has never really learned to stay alone at home. That's why I would like to strongly recommend to every dog-owner to teach that to his dog. Even if our dog is allowed to come with us in most cases, it may happen that he must stay alone.

Apropos Dog Accessories

I have to say it because I keep noticing how much money people spend on dog accessories. There are winter coats, raincoats, snowshoes and many things more. Some accessories may even make sense and provide protection for the dog. So, it's quite purposeful to use shiny collars or ropes. Actually, these things are useful in the winter season and your dog is being seen by others more clearly. It happened to me that a dog crossed the street just before me. Hadn't he had that flashing light attacked to his collar, I would have hit him with my car because I saw his body much too late in the darkness.

That's why these products are a good investment, since they provide protection in the dark season. Only a few days ago, I found hi-vis vests in a pet supplies shop. Well, basically no bad idea, especially if worn by animals with a long fur. The flashing lights and shiny collars are hardly visible, if your pet has got a long and thick fur.

But I'm really shocked at seeing all that clothing for smaller dogs. Clothing, pants and many products more. That's a humanization of dogs and is absolutely nonsensical. Some time ago, I mentioned that subject to our vet because our Chi freezes quite easily in winter. He's built close to the ground, has got short fur, no undercoat at all, and, apart from that, is rather small-boned. The vet even recommended to me to pull a dog coat over the dog in winter or in rain. Simply because it wouldn't be long before our Chi would get a cystitis - or kidney inflammation, which he had two times before.

Talking to the vet, I came to the conclusion that dog coats are recommended to be worn by dogs with short fur and no undercoat. Generally speaking, this clothing would be harmful, since humidity is being stored underneath them and can easily cause rheumatism. That was my vet's reply. He recommends dog clothing for the cold and rainy season, but only for old or weakened dogs, animals with a very short fur and no undercoat or dogs suffering from rheumatism that have trouble tolerating damp wetness. After wearing the fur should be rubbed dry with a hand towel, so the dog won't start freezing through the wet skin.

Moreover, I consulted people on winter shoes. We've got that problem with our Chi: The salt on his paws is burning, and when it's very cold outside, he would always try to pull in one leg because he's freezing. I used to rub his paws with vaseline and clean them carefully with lukewarm water when back from our walks. Even my vet wouldn't favour these winter shoes. In the meantime, however, I had the chance to see some dogs walking with these shoes downtown, and the expression "walking" is almost exaggerated. It was more of a waddle and pulling in of legs because the dogs considered these shoes a foreign body. So, I think a dog won't like these shoes at all. My vet further told me that these shoes could be quite purposeful, if you're out with your dog in temperatures way below zero for a long time. Okay, I think every dog-owner has to decide for himself and his dog.

But please, dear dog-owners, only use clothing for your dogs, if it's absolutely necessary. Even a Chihuahua doesn't need to wear a little dress when it's summer just because it looks so cute. The dog's sweating and can even suffer from a heat stroke. With all due respect to the cuteness of all these accessories for dogs, always make up your mind, if it's really needed. Your dog is not a little puppet, but a living being. And every dog has got his natural instincts and doesn't want to be treated like a human. Your dog is not a substitute for a child!

Right at the moment, people make a lot of money with that sort of product, all the more Chihuahuas seem to be rather trendy at present. No question, it's the perfect dog, he doesn't need much space and is small enough to fit into a handbag. But that's not the place these little cuties want to be in. They want to be running freely, romping about and sniffing around. Rest assured, no dog wants to be carried in a handbag.

Of course, I like to carry my dog on the arm, particularly when walking in an area where there are many people. Reason being that people are often careless and may tread down the dog. But normally, he's a real dog that likes running and exploring his world.

If you buy stuff for your dog, take a good browse through the product range and only buy what he really needs. Basically, he wouldn't need a lot for grooming and keeping, except for a well-fitted breast harness which is important and which wouldn't restrict him in any way. Furthermore, you need a leash and, of course, food and food bowls. Perhaps a brush, should your dog have long fur. Also, you should have a mild dog shampoo, if he gets dirtier than usual. Then, of course, there is need for his basket and a basket to be placed inside the car where he can sit down. That's it. The equipment is rather manageable, and as far as toys are concerned, you will buy them here and there anyway because, be sure, his teeth will have disassembled things in no time.

I sincerely hope I could open your eyes a bit. Always bear in mind that clothing can have the opposite effect and make your dog sick.

Closing Remarks

There are many different opinions on dog education, and every dog-owner has his own predilections. In my view, it's important to listen to all of these opinions and, provided your dog won't be hurt or made insecure, you're invited to test the various methods of dog education yourself.

Always bear in mind that dog education must be without violence and without screaming at the dog. The dog has no interest in bugging you, he just wants to learn and to live the life of a dog, which he can do, if you let him. A happy and contented dog is a great companion and a family member for many years.

My Chi is approaching his tenth year of his life and will be counted among the senior dogs soon. But I also love to think back to our first dog that died years ago. Once you've lost your heart to a dog, there is nothing you can do anymore. A dog can give you so much - and as I said before, just have a look at these ingenuous eyes, and you will feel like looking right into his soul.

All that remains to be said is that I'm wishing you all the best, all success you need, and much fun with your four-legged friend.

Did you enjoy this Book?

Dear Readers,

Are you happy with this book? Is it meeting your expectations?

If yes, I'm looking forward to receiving your messages, your praise, your criticism, and your suggestions.

I would be pleased, if you left feedback on Amazon to give me the chance to improve.

Thank you in advance!

Cordially yours,

Janna Hellenbeck

Disclaimer

The implementation of all information, instructions and strategies contained in this book is at your own risk. The author cannot be held liable for any damages of any kind for any legal reason. Liability claims against the author for material or non-material damages caused by the use or non-use of the information or by the use of incorrect and/or incomplete information are excluded in principle. Therefore, any legal and damage claims are also excluded. This work was compiled and written down with the greatest care and to the best of our knowledge. However, the author accepts no responsibility for the topicality, completeness and quality of the information. Printing errors and misinformation cannot be completely excluded. No legal responsibility or liability of any kind can be assumed for incorrect information provided by the author.

Copyright

Impressum

© Janna Hellenbeck
2023
1st edition

All rights reserved.

Reprinting, even in extracts, is not permitted.

No part of this work may be reproduced, duplicated or distributed in any form without the written permission of the author.

Contact us: Mark Lipke, Kuhanger 9, 31787 Hameln-Germany
Cover design: B.M.
Cover:Deposit

Printed in Great Britain
by Amazon

22660364R00152